# H. P. BLAVATSKY
and the SPR

# H. P. BLAVATSKY and the SPR

An Examination of the Hodgson Report of 1885

by

Vernon Harrison, Ph.D.

*Member of The Society for Psychical Research*
LONDON, ENGLAND

THEOSOPHICAL UNIVERSITY PRESS
PASADENA, CALIFORNIA

THEOSOPHICAL UNIVERSITY PRESS
POST OFFICE BOX C
PASADENA, CALIFORNIA 91109-7107
1997

Copyright © 1997 by Theosophical University Press

All rights including the right of reproduction in whole or in part in any form are reserved under International and Pan-American Copyright Conventions.

The paper in this book is acid-free and meets the standards for permanence of the Council on Library Resources.

**Library of Congress Cataloging-in-Publication Data**

Harrison, Vernon, 1912–
    H. P. Blavatsky and the SPR : an examination of the Hodgson report of 1885 / by Vernon Harrison
    p.    cm.
    ISBN 1-55700-117-0 (cloth : alk. paper)
    ISBN 1-55700-118-9 (pbk : alk. paper)

    1. Blavatsky, H. P. (Helena Petrovna), 1831–1891.   2. Society for Psychical Research (London, England).   3. Parapsychology — Investigation.   4. Hodgson, Richard, 1855–1905.   5. Theosophy. I. Title.

BP585.B6H28   1997
299′.934′092—dc21                                           97-9329
                                                                                  CIP

Printed at Theosophical University Press
Pasadena, California

# Contents

| | |
|---|---|
| About This Book | vii |
| Acknowledgments | xiii |
| **PART 1** | |
|    J'Accuse: | 3 |
|    An Examination of the | |
|    Hodgson Report of 1885 | |
| **PART 2** | |
|    J'Accuse d'autant plus: | 37 |
|    A Further Study of | |
|    the Hodgson Report | |
| Replies to Criticism | 61 |
| Opinion | 67 |
| Affidavit | 73 |
| About the Author | 77 |

# About This Book

BLAVATSKY, HELENA PETROVNA, born Helena Petrovna Hahn, 1831-1891, Russian theosophist. She . . . founded the Theosophical Society in New York [in 1875]. Her demonstrations of supernormal phenomena were declared fraudulent by the London Society for Psychical Research (1885).
— *Reader's Digest Universal Dictionary*,
reprinted with amendments, 1994

This statement, typical of many, is factually correct — as far as it goes. The damage done lies not in what is said, but in what is left unsaid. As Patience Worth aptly has it:

Half-Truth is Lie's brother.

The "REPORT OF THE COMMITTEE APPOINTED TO INVESTIGATE PHENOMENA CONNECTED WITH THE THEOSOPHICAL SOCIETY" appeared in 1885 in the *Proceedings of the Society for Psychical Research,* Vol. 3 (December 1885), pp. 201-400. It is commonly called the Hodgson Report since the bulk of it was written by R. Hodgson; but his opinions were endorsed by E. Gurney, F. W. H. Myers, F. Podmore, H. Sidgwick, Mrs. Sidgwick and J. H. Stack. It branded Madame H. P. Blavatsky, founder of the Theosophical Society, as "one of the most accomplished, ingenious, and interesting impostors in history." This view is still widely accepted, although it is probable that few have ever read the Hodgson Report critically and in detail, and fewer still have attempted to check his findings. Among many other accusations, the Hodgson Report claims that Madame Blavatsky herself wrote in a disguised hand certain letters commonly called the Mahatma Letters, and that she was engaged in forgery and deception on an impressive scale.

Although much of the evidence relating to this case has been lost and all the witnesses are long since dead, many of the Mahatma Letters to A. P. Sinnett are preserved in the British Library where they are available for inspection. *These letters make Primary Evidence.* A study of these originals, supplemented by a detailed examination of an authentic set of 1,323 color slides prepared from them and supplied by the British Library, has shown that there are serious flaws in Hodgson's methods, observation, reasoning, and conclusions.

This book is divided into two parts. Part 1 reprints my earlier paper entitled "J'Accuse," published in the *Journal of the Society for Psychical Research,* Vol. 53, No. 803 (April 1986), pp. 286-310, plus a few footnotes for clarity's sake. This is, in the main, a study of the Hodgson Report itself, supplemented by as detailed a study of the Mahatma Letters as time and opportunity to visit the British Library permitted. It is reproduced here because the *Journal of the Society for Psychical Research* does not circulate widely outside the SPR and some libraries.

Part 2 describes work done after 1986 and records the findings of a line-by-line microscopical examination of each and every one of the 1,323 color slides in the British Library set. Several pages of these documents are reproduced in this book. Hodgson gave no illustration whatever of the alleged incriminating Blavatsky-Coulomb letters, of which he made much; and the only illustrations of the Mahatma Letters given in his Report are fragments, mostly isolated characters torn from their context and from documents which, for the most part, can neither be identified nor accurately dated.

In "J'Accuse" I wrote: "whereas Hodgson was prepared to use any evidence, however trivial or questionable, to implicate HPB, he ignored all evidence that could be used in her favor. His report is riddled with slanted statements, conjectures advanced as fact or probable fact, uncorroborated testimony of unnamed witnesses, selection of evidence and downright falsity." If this seem hyperbole, I reply that now that I have had the opportunity of re-reading the Hodgson Report in the light of the hard evidence that still remains to us (i.e., the Mahatma Letters preserved in the British Library), the Hodgson Report is even worse than I had thought. The Hodgson Report is not, as has been widely believed for more than a century, a model of what impartial and painstaking research should be: it is the work of a man who has reached his conclusions early on in his investigation and thereafter, selecting and distorting evidence, did not hesitate to adopt flawed arguments to support his thesis.

My conclusions from this examination are:

FIRST: The Hodgson Report is not a scientific study. It is more like the address of a counsel for the prosecution who is interested only in evidence, however dubious, which can be made to support his views. Hodgson shows that he was either ignorant or contemptuous of the basic principles of English justice — and the rest of the Committee seemed little better. As said, he quotes verbal and uncorroborated statements of unnamed witnesses; he cites documents which are neither reproduced in his report nor identifiable; he advances conjecture as established fact; and he makes his handwriting experts change their minds until they give him the answers he wants. The possibility that someone other than HPB could have written the Mahatma Letters was never considered. This list of misdemeanors alone would render the Hodgson Report inadmissible in a court of law.

SECOND: In cases where it has been possible to check Hodgson's statements against the direct testimony of the Letters preserved in the British Library, his statements are found to be either false or of no significance in the context. He makes three cardinal statements on which hangs his whole contention that Madame Blavatsky wrote the Mahatma Letters herself with intent to deceive. These I summarize as follows:

(i) That there are clear signs of development in the KH handwriting, various strong resemblances to Madame Blavatsky's ordinary handwriting having been gradually eliminated;

(ii) That special forms of letters proper to Madame Blavatsky's ordinary writing, and not proper to the KH writing, occasionally appear in the latter;

(iii) That there are certain very marked peculiarities of Madame Blavatsky's ordinary writing which appear throughout the KH writing.

The first two are demonstrably false; the third could apply to many other writers and does not pinpoint HPB as the writer to the exclusion of all other possible writers. These downright falsities coupled with the procedural errors, make it impossible for me to accept as a fair, impartial statement of fact those parts of the Hodgson Report that I *can* verify from primary evidence. This being so, I may perhaps be pardoned for regarding with suspicion the remainder of the Hodgson Report for which supporting firsthand evidence is no longer extant.

THIRD: The KH and M scripts raise unanswered questions about whether they were written by pen and ink (or blue pencil) on paper in the ordinary way. These questions relate to

(i) The extraordinary striations, made with engineering precision, in some of the Letters apparently written in blue pencil;

(ii) The small amount of ink penetration even with the thinnest papers;

(iii) Erasures that seem to have been made with ink eradicator, but which have left neither stain nor roughening of the paper;

(iv) The distortions in some pages of writing which otherwise bear all the marks of genuine KH writing. Of these, the most conspicuous are the exaggerated t-bars which are seen in some of the later KH Letters.

All of these points suggest that the Letters we have are copies, made by some unknown process, rather than original documents, but only laboratory investigation can provide an answer. I have long sought to have some nondestructive laboratory tests made, but without success; and I fear that it is unlikely that permission to do such work will be forthcoming.

LAST: I find *no evidence of common origin* of the KH and M scripts and HPB's ordinary, consciously-made handwriting. That is to say, I find no evidence that the Mahatma Letters were written by Madame Blavatsky in a disguised form of her ordinary writing made for fraudulent purposes. What may have come through her hand in trance, dislocation, or other forms of altered consciousness is another matter; but writing so made cannot be classed as either fraud or imposture.

If there is insufficient evidence in the legal sense, a case must be dropped; for in English law a person is innocent until he is proved guilty and a "not proven" verdict is not allowed. Remember that the charge against HPB made by Hodgson was that she was an accomplished but nevertheless common fraudster and impostor.

I have done this work impelled by a strong feeling of the need for JUSTICE. This is a concept that seems beyond the grasp of some parapsychologists and psychical researchers. Mediumistic people are not just objects that can be used for "experiments." The lasting damage that can be done to their lives by a hasty or erroneous judgment must always be considered.

In the course of my practical work I am often called upon to advise in the defense of dubious characters, some of whom may have served prison sentences. The fact that they have a "record" does not mean they can, ipso facto, be convicted of each and every charge that may subsequently be brought against them. They cannot be condemned "on suspicion." Each verdict must be based upon the available evidence pertaining to that case and not on previous history.

H. P. Blavatsky was not a known criminal and had not served a prison sentence. Yet Hodgson was allowed to act as both Expert Witness and Public Prosecutor. There was no Counsel for the Defense, no cross-examination of Hodgson's favored witnesses or recall of witnesses whom he had rejected, no Judge and no Jury. The meanest criminal in the courts can expect fairer treatment than was ever accorded Madame Blavatsky at the hands of the SPR; and the Hodgson Report has been allowed to become one of the most sacred of all the SPR's sacred cows, as I have discovered.

I joined the SPR in 1937 and have been in continuous membership ever since. This must make me one of the Society's most senior members. In recent years I have contributed on a regular basis to the Society's *Journal* and one volume of *Proceedings*. I joined the SPR as a young man hoping that it could answer for me those age-old problems: the Whence, the Whither, the Why. I have come to share the experience of Omar Khayyám, as related in Fitzgerald's famous lines:

> Myself when young did eagerly frequent
> Doctor and Saint, and heard great Argument
>    About it and about: but evermore
> Came out by the same Door as in I went.
>
> With them the Seed of Wisdom did I sow
> And with my own hand labour'd it to grow:
>    And this was all the Harvest that I reap'd —
> "I came like Water, and like Wind I go."

And yet, with all the aridity of so many of the SPR's publications, the Society has provided me with four fine tutors who have influenced my development greatly. They never knew me, but I remember them with affection and gratitude: C. D. Broad, H. H. Price, R. H. Thouless, and G. N. M. Tyrrell.

I am not a member of the Theosophical Society, though I can subscribe to the three principles on which it was founded.* I have read much of Theosophical literature, in its several brands, but I do not know how much of it may be true. However, I have found some Theosophical teaching useful in explaining facts that I cannot otherwise account for. Ideas which I have borrowed include: the sevenfold nature of man; the difference between individuality and personality; the persistence and reactivation of kama-manasic shells; and karma and rebirth. H. P. Blavatsky for me is a writer and source of ideas; and she takes her place with George Berkeley, Bishop of Cloyne; Swedenborg; Swedenborg's irreverent disciple, William Blake; and Carl Jung.

H. P. Blavatsky wrote: "he who hears an innocent person slandered, whether a brother theosophist or not, and does not undertake his defense as he would undertake his own — is no Theosophist" (*Lucifer*, November 1887). Maybe, on this criterion, I am a theosophist.

The results of the present investigation, which has been extended over a fifteen-year period, are now presented in the hope that future biographers of Madame H. P. Blavatsky, the compilers of reference books, encyclopedias and dictionaries, as well as the general public, will come to realize that the Hodgson Report is not the model of impartial investigation so often claimed for it over the past century. It is flawed and untrustworthy; and Hodgson's observations and conclusions need to be taken with a considerable portion of salt.

The case of Helena Petrovna Blavatsky needs re-examination in this light. She deserves no less.

VERNON HARRISON

21 March 1997

---

*1) To form a nucleus of a Universal Brotherhood of Humanity, without distinction of race, creed, sex, caste or color;
2) To study ancient and modern religions, philosophies, and sciences, and to demonstrate the importance of such study; and
3) To investigate the unexplained laws of Nature and the powers latent in man.

# Acknowledgments

Grateful acknowledgment goes to the Society for Psychical Research for permission to reproduce "J'Accuse" as Part 1 of the present study; and to the British Library for permission to reproduce full color photographs of the Mahatma Letters (Additional MSS 45284, 45285, 45286).

Figures 5 and 8 are reproduced by permission from *You Are What You Write* by Huntington Hartford, published by Peter Owen Limited, London, 1975.

I am indebted to the Trustees of the British Museum for permission to quote the information provided by the Archivist about Mr. Richard Sims, formerly on the staff of the Museum.

I am obliged to Ambassador John S. D. Eisenhower for kindly lending me a fine specimen of the late President Eisenhower's handwriting.

I have received valuable information in private letters from Anita Atkins, the late Walter A. Carrithers, Jr., and Michael Gomes. Their contributions are referred to in the text.

Michael Gomes has searched independently for the originals of the Blavatsky-Coulomb letters and confirms that they were never used by Coues in his defense and are now lost. The evidence that these letters were indeed forgeries — and that in consequence the testimony of the Coulombs was quite unreliable — is now very strong. Hodgson accepts the Coulombs' testimony almost without question, and if this has to be discounted, much of his case collapses.

Walter Carrithers has examined in great detail the contradictory statements made by Hodgson and Madame Coulomb in connection with the "shrine" and other apparatus alleged to have been used in the production of phenomena, but I have not attempted to examine this aspect of the case in the present work.

I thank the Archivist of the Theosophical Society, Pasadena, for the extended loan of the set of 1,323 color slides of the Mahatma Letters first published by A. Trevor Barker in the 1920s, and Theosophical University Press for undertaking the publication of my findings.

Last, but not least, I am ever grateful to Elsie, my wife and constant companion of nearly fifty years, without whose support and understanding it is unlikely that these monographs would ever have been written.

PART 1

# J'Accuse

Qui Vult Caedere Canem Facile Invenit Fustem
(He who wants to beat a dog readily finds a stick)

PART 1

# J'Accuse*

## An Examination of the Hodgson Report of 1885

*Editorial Note* to Vernon Harrison's article "J'Accuse"

In December 1885, The Society for Psychical Research [SPR] published in its Proceedings *(Part IX, pp. 201-400) the* "Report of the Committee appointed to Investigate Phenomena Connected with the Theosophical Society." *The Committee consisted of: E. Gurney, F. W. H. Myers, F. Podmore, H. Sidgwick, J. H. Stack, R. Hodgson and Mrs. H. Sidgwick. The main bulk of this publication was the account written by Richard Hodgson who, at the behest of the Society, had gone to India to investigate further the activities of Mme. Helena Petrovna Blavatsky, co-founder with Col. H. S. Olcott, in 1875, of the Theosophical Society. Mme. Blavatsky was credited with a variety of paranormal phenomena but the Committee, in their Conclusions, accuse her of gross fraud and of being an impostor. Although, as it has been repeatedly pointed out, The SPR holds no corporate opinions, it has widely been regarded as responsible for endorsing the "Hodgson Report" (as we shall hereafter refer to the report as a whole) and hence as being on record as condemning Mme. Blavatsky. Members of the Theosophical Society have, naturally, resented this slur on the good name of their founder and have repeatedly challenged the Report's conclusions. For many years, Walter A. Carrithers, not a member of the Theosophical Society but a long-standing member of the SPR who has written extensively on the case, some of which is published under the pen name "Adlai Waterman," has campaigned to get the SPR Council to disown, publicly, the Report. In April 1983, Mr. Leslie Price, a member of the SPR Library Committee and, since January 1985, editor of the new quarterly* Theosophical History, *gave one of the SPR Lectures with the title: "Madame Blavatsky Unveiled?" (which is to be published early in 1986 by the Theosophical History Centre) in which he, too, criticizes Hodgson's methods and arguments. In this issue of our Journal, coming as it does almost exactly one hundred years after the publication of the Hodgson*

---

*"J'Accuse" — title of Emile Zola's celebrated open letter to the President of the French Republic concerning the Dreyfus case.

Report, we are happy, in the interests of truth and fair play, and to make amends for whatever offense we may have given, to publish here one such critical analysis by a handwriting expert. His expertise is of special relevance in this instance since much of the Hodgson Report concerns the authorship of certain letters which Hodgson claims were forged by Mme. Blavatsky herself. Dr. Vernon Harrison, a past President of the Royal Photographic Society, was, for ten years, Research Manager to Thomas De La Rue, printers of banknotes, passports and stamps, etc., so there is probably not much that he does not know about forgery. He is not a member of the Theosophical Society but he is a long-standing member of the SPR. Whether readers agree or disagree with his conclusions, we are pleased to offer him the hospitality of our columns and we hope that, hereafter, Theosophists, and, indeed, all who care for the reputation of Helena Petrovna Blavatsky, will look upon us in a more kindly light. — THE EDITOR [John Beloff, Ph.D.]

The "REPORT OF THE COMMITTEE APPOINTED TO INVESTIGATE PHENOMENA CONNECTED WITH THE THEOSOPHICAL SOCIETY" (commonly called the Hodgson Report) is the most celebrated and controversial of all the reports published by the Society for Psychical Research. It passes judgment on Madame H. P. Blavatsky, the founder of Theosophy; and the final sentence in the "Statement and Conclusions of the Committee" has been quoted in book after book, encyclopedia after encyclopedia, without hint that it might be wrong. It runs:

> For our own part, we regard her neither as the mouthpiece of hidden seers, nor as a mere vulgar adventuress; we think that she has achieved a title to permanent remembrance as one of the most accomplished, ingenious, and interesting impostors in history. — p. 207

For years Hodgson has been presented as an example of a perfect psychical researcher, and his report a model of what a report on psychical research should be.

I shall show that, on the contrary, the Hodgson Report is a highly partisan document forfeiting all claim to scientific impartiality. It is the address of a Counsel for the Prosecution who does not hesitate to select evidence to suit his case, ignoring and suppressing everything that tends to contradict his thesis. The Counsel for the Defense was never heard.

I make no attempt in this paper to prove that Madame Blavatsky was guiltless of charges preferred against her. At this distance of time, when all witnesses are dead and much of the evidence has been lost or destroyed, this would be difficult if not impossible. Nor do I attempt to establish the authorship or appraise the content of the *Mahatma Letters*. To do so is a fascinating but formidably difficult task. My present objective is a more limited one: to demonstrate that the case against Madame Blavatsky in the Hodgson Report is NOT PROVEN — in the Scots sense.

## HISTORICAL

Madame Blavatsky's brush with the psychical researchers started with the Coulomb affair. This has been described many times from various points of view, and I need but outline events here. It seems that HPB and Madame Coulomb first met in Cairo about 1871. The Coulombs became bankrupt, had to leave, and turned up at Bombay in 1880, penniless and homeless, appealing to HPB for help. She gave them home and shelter, and positions of trust. Madame Coulomb became housekeeper and her husband acted as general factotum.

On 20 February 1884, HPB and Colonel Olcott left for Europe, entrusting the management of the Theosophical Society to a Board of Control. In March, the Board of Control found the Coulombs guilty of gross misconduct. They were dismissed on 14 May.

We next hear of them in the *Madras Christian College Magazine*. Selections of letters were published which, if genuine and interpreted correctly, would prove conspiracy in trickery between Madame Blavatsky and the Coulombs. HPB claimed that the letters were, at least in part, forgeries. In addition to these, a forged letter purporting to be written by Dr. Hartmann to Madame Coulomb, dated 28 April 1884, is asserted by Colonel Olcott to have reached him some weeks later in an envelope addressed in an unknown hand and bearing the Madras postmark, but the forger is not known.

While he was in England, Colonel Olcott made friendly contact with leading members of the Society for Psychical Research who were interested in reports of phenomena produced by HPB, and in May of 1884 the Council of the SPR appointed a committee to examine the evidence for the alleged phenomena. The members of this committee were: E. Gurney, F. W. H. Myers, F. Podmore, Henry Sidgwick, and J. H. Stack — with the later addition of Mrs. Sidgwick and R. Hodgson. The committee was able to examine Madame Blavatsky, Colonel Olcott, Mohini M. Chatterji and Mr. Sinnett. The result of their inquiries was published in *First Report of the Committee*, issued in 1884 for the private information of members of the SPR only. I have no quarrel with this report. It seems that the examination was carried out courteously and at the end the committee did not know what to think. The phenomena described seemed to be so remarkable and outside ordinary experience that they could be received only with strong reservations; on the other hand, the number of witnesses and the strength of the testimony were such that the evidence could not be dismissed lightly. They decided that there was a good case for further investigation.

This further investigation was made by Richard Hodgson during a three-months' visit to India. The final *Report of the Committee*, issued in *Proceedings*, Part IX, December 1885, is virtually Hodgson's report, since the rest of the committee did little more than rubber-stamp his conclusions. They made no attempt to correct glaring errors of procedure or to check critically Hodgson's findings.

THE BLAVATSKY-COULOMB LETTERS

The Blavatsky-Coulomb letters published by the *Christian College Magazine* are of prime importance since, *if* they are genuine and *if* they can be taken at their face value, they prove that HPB was engaged in fraudulent activities; and we need go no further. There seem to be only two possibilities:

(a) that HPB was engaged in fraud on a gigantic scale, involving a number of confederates, and was denounced by the Coulombs in disgust;

(b) that the Coulombs forged the incriminating letters in order to bring about HPB's downfall.

In considering these alternatives, one must take into account the possible motives of the participants.

If HPB was engaged in fraud on a vast scale involving many confederates, then even Hodgson had to admit that none of the usual motives for fraud applied. The best that he could suggest was that she was a Russian agent set to "foster and foment as widely as possible among the natives a disaffection towards British rule." In the 1980s when Russian agents are two a penny, this idea does not pull: there are more effective ways of promoting Russian interests in Afghanistan than by writing *Isis Unveiled* or forging the Mahatma Letters.

On the other hand, if the Coulombs forged the letters, their motive is clear: the primitive and powerful one of *revenge*. Having been dismissed under a cloud, they had lost both home and employment.

The point I stress is that, if Madame Blavatsky was suspect, so also were the Coulombs. Correct procedure requires that the *incriminating portions* of the Blavatsky-Coulomb letters should be reproduced in the report together with acknowledged specimens of the handwriting of Madame Blavatsky, Mr. Coulomb, and Madame Coulomb. This was never done; and it is omission inexcusable. We should also note that Madame Coulomb was, in modern terminology, a "supergrass"*; and the testimony of such should be received with caution.

It is now morally certain that the originals of the incriminating Blavatsky-Coulomb letters have been destroyed. They are not in the archives of the Christian College at Madras, nor are they in the archives of the Theosophical Society at Adyar. I am much indebted to Anita Atkins of New York for the following information:

> The last known recipient of the HPB-Coulomb letters was Professor Elliott Coues, Smithsonian scientist, and ex-theosophist, who turned against HPB, and gave a ferociously slanderous 7 column interview on her in the *New York Sun* in 1890. HPB sued for libel; the *Sun's* investigation and that of its lawyers found HPB had been slandered, and were about to award her damages, when she died. This under New York libel law ended the suit. But the *Sun* nevertheless publicly and editorially retracted.
>
> During this period when Coues was fighting the suit, he bought the Coulomb letters, through an agent of the Scottish missionaries in India. I have a photostatic copy of his check. It is contained in the Coues archives at the State Historical Society of Wisconsin, Madison, Wisconsin. I have a microfilm of all his papers on theosophy and related matters. The Coulomb letters are NOT in the archives. Now Coues' purpose in acquiring the letters was to obtain evidence for his defense of HPB's suit, to prove her a fraud. His wife was a millionairess, and consequently he had every professional means available to overthrow HPB, if these letters were genuine.
>
> However, complete silence — he never mentioned he had them. He either destroyed them during his life, or left instructions for his heir to destroy them.

---

*["Grass": British slang. An informer, esp. a police informer. "Supergrass": A member of a criminal gang who turns police informer on the others and expects concessions in return. — V.H.]

Walter A. Carrithers has this to add:

> About 1948 I procured a copy of the last Will of Professor Coues, and proceeded to search out his living posterity — only to learn that one of them, then but recently deceased, had pitched into his fireplace what was described as "many letters" ostensibly written by the hand of Madame Blavatsky; and, of all places, his residence had been just a way upstate from Fresno (so that I could have visited him on any day and determined what these were *before* their destruction!) in Palo Alto, California.

The circumstantial evidence that the Blavatsky-Coulomb letters were found after expert examination to be forgeries is strong.

No facsimile of any of the incriminating letters is given in the Hodgson Report. Hodgson explains that he had sent a selection (to wit, *his* selection) of the letters to F. G. Netherclift for a professional opinion, but found on his return to England that the letters had already been sent back to Madras, so that he could not make facsimiles of them. This is an unacceptable excuse. The letters were a vital part of the evidence. Photography was well advanced in 1884. There were good professional photographers operating in the Madras area who would have made accurate and permanent copies of these important documents. The handwriting of the Coulombs was never examined by Netherclift or by any other competent person.

Hodgson treats the whole matter very lightly and says:

> I do not propose to go into any detail in describing the similarities between Madame Blavatsky's undoubted handwriting and the handwriting of the Blavatsky-Coulomb letters. These letters, before publication in the *Christian College Magazine,* were, as I have said, submitted by the editor to several gentlemen with experience in handwriting, who were unequivocally of opinion that they were written by Madame Blavatsky. The same opinion was also expressed by Mr. J. D. B. Gribble, of Madras, in "A Report of an Examination into the Blavatsky Correspondence, published in the *Christian College Magazine.*" But the most important judgment on this point is that of the expert on handwriting, Mr. F. G. Netherclift, who has no doubt whatever that the disputed letters which were submitted to him were written by Madame Blavatsky. His report will be found on p. 381. Mr. Sims, of the British Museum, is also of the same opinion.
>
> Under these circumstances I need say little more than that I examined the whole of these documents, and throughout I found those characteristics of Madame Blavatsky's handwriting which were present in the document I

used as my chief standard, *viz.*, a letter from Madame Blavatsky to Dr. Hartmann, written from Elberfeld in October, 1884. — pp. 276–7

To this I have to reply:

(a) The reported opinions of certain unnamed gentlemen are not evidence. Gribble tells us that the said gentlemen had experience in banking, not handwriting. No professional expert was available.

(b) We shall see later that Hodgson rejects Gribble's testimony *in toto* when it suits him. He cannot have it both ways.

(c) We have not a single written statement from Mr. Sims of the British Museum, only Hodgson's reports of what he said or thought.

It follows that the only independent testimony of any weight that we have is Netherclift's Report, reproduced (in part) on pages 381 and 382 of the Hodgson Report.

Mr. Sims of the British Museum

Mr. Sims of the British Museum is a shadowy figure who seems to do little more than echo the changeable opinions of Netherclift. I am grateful for the following information about him provided by the Archivist of the British Museum.

Mr. Richard Sims was the son of one of the senior servants at Wadham College, Oxford, and was educated at New College School (not New College itself). He joined the established staff of the British Museum in 1841 and resigned from the staff in 1887. He was proficient in Latin, Greek, French, and English, and had some knowledge of Spanish and German. He could read ancient writings with facility. He was appointed in the Department of Manuscripts as a Transcriber and became Assistant (First Class) in 1879. In a testimonial to his abilities, E. A. Bond, Keeper of Manuscripts at the Museum, stated that he was able to describe Charters and ordinary manuscripts in French and Latin, and that he could be serviceably employed in cataloguing charters and certain classes of manuscripts, such as those of Topography, Genealogy, and Heraldry.

There is thus no reason to doubt Sims' competence and integrity; but he was not a specialist in forgeries, and the fact remains that we have no direct written statements from him. We do not know whether his opinions were given verbally or in writing, and what exactly was asked of him. There is little prospect now that we shall ever locate his original letters or reports.

## Netherclift's Report

Netherclift's Report is a curious document in several respects.

(a) The title appended to it runs: "Report of Mr. F. G. Netherclift, Expert in Handwriting, on the Blavatsky-Coulomb Documents." This is misleading, for Netherclift was sent only a selection — Hodgson's own selection — of these documents. The Report itself is mutilated, part being excised; and it carries two dates.

(b) Netherclift starts his report: "In compliance with your instructions, I have carefully examined . . ." We are not told what these instructions were. Was Netherclift instructed to look for skillful fraudulent alterations to, or interpolations in, otherwise genuine letters? Or did he make a cursory inspection of the documents as a whole? We do not know.

Netherclift merely makes an *ex cathedra* pronouncement that the letters (whatever they may have been) were all written by Madame Blavatsky. What he should have demonstrated, giving his detailed reasons, was that the incriminating portions of the letters were in the genuine handwriting of Madame Blavatsky. No reference is made to any incriminating portions.

(c) Worst of all, the documents submitted to Netherclift cannot be identified. This is remarkable, since an Examiner needs, in his own interest, to state what his instructions were and to identify clearly the documents submitted to him for examination. This statement should form an integral part of the report — lest an unscrupulous client use the report to cover documents that have not been examined, with possible legal trouble later on.

Netherclift states that he had received two packets. With the exception of a slip of paper with writing commencing "Damodar send me," all the letters in Packet 2 were sent to Mr. Myers and are not in dispute.

Packet 1 is stated by Netherclift to have contained the following:

(a) Envelope marked 3 containing a slip of paper, the writing on which commences, "The Mahatma has heard . . ."

(b) A telegram in a different handwriting.

(c) An envelope addressed to Madame E. Coulomb.

(d) A letter on green paper.

(e) A letter on pink paper.

(f) Envelope marked 7 containing a scrap of ruled paper marked 10, the writing on which commences, "La poste . . ."

(g) Envelope directed [to] Madame and Monsieur Coulomb.

(h) Envelope marked 10 containing a letter marked 2, the writing on which commences, "Ma belle chère amie . . ."

(i) Envelope marked 28 containing a letter of several pages written in violet ink.

(j) Envelope marked No. 11 containing a letter in violet ink commencing, "Ma chère Madame Coulomb . . ."

The *envelopes* in PACKET 1 could have contained anything and are useless as evidence. The telegram, whatever it was, was not in Madame Blavatsky's handwriting. On pages 211-216 of the Hodgson Report, Hodgson gives fourteen extracts from the Blavatsky-Coulomb correspondence. Nine of these extracts carry an asterisk, which we are told means that "the letters from which these extracts are taken were among those examined by Mr. Netherclift." It is however impossible to relate them to the documents listed in Netherclift's PACKET 1.

The slip of paper starting, "The Mahatma has heard . . ." can be identified, and the text is not incriminating. We do not know what the letters on green and pink paper were nor, for that matter, to whom they were addressed.

Item (f), the slip of paper with the words starting, "La poste . . ." seems to be Hodgson's extract 12, which runs:

> La poste part ma chère. Je n'ai qu'un instant. Votre lettre arrivée trop tard. Oui, laissez Srinavas Rao se prosterner devant le *shrine* et s'il demande ou non, je vous supplie lui faire passer cette reponse par K.H. car il s'y attend; *je sais ce qu'il veut.* Demain vous aurez une grande lettre! Grandes nouvelles! Merci. H.P.B. — p. 215

This chit seems to contain nothing more sinister than a hasty instruction to Madame Coulomb to allow Mr. Sreenevas Rao to pay his respects to the "shrine" and to make sure that he gets the enclosed letter from KH which he is expecting. Nothing miraculous is suggested.

Item (h) cannot be related to any of the starred extracts: none of them starts, "Ma belle chère amie . . ." Item (i) cannot be positively identified, but it may be the one dated 1 April 1884 which Gribble had noted as "by far the longest of any published" and which was written in purple, or violet, ink. If so, it was "partly defiant and partly imploring," but it contained no admission of guilt. Item (j) cannot be identified.

If we reject the envelopes and telegram in PACKET 1, we are left with two scraps of paper and five letters. Thus two, at least, of the starred extracts remain unaccounted for. These presumably were included in a completely unspecified "second batch of Blavatsky-Coulomb letters" submitted "shortly afterwards" to Mr. Netherclift. The documents sent in this "second batch" are not listed, nor have we any formal report on them; all we have is Hodgson's assertion that Netherclift returned them with a blanket endorsement on the cover in which they had been sent. Such laxity on the part of a professional expert is hard to credit, since letters could be removed from, or inserted into, this cover at any time without fear of detection.

We note also that of all the documents included in PACKET 1, five certainly, and possibly a sixth, were not incriminating. We are entitled to wonder therefore whether Netherclift examined *any* of the incriminating passages which might have been interpolated into otherwise genuine letters. We must also ask why his procedure was so lax and irregular.

THE MAHATMA LETTERS

The Mahatma Letters are attributed to more than one author. Hodgson confines his attention to the most important series of letters — the "Koot Hoomi" or "KH" scripts — and claims that he has established from his examination, confirmed by experts in handwriting, that HPB wrote the Mahatma Letters except those which he admits she could not possibly have written. These latter, he asserts, were written by confederates.

Two general points need first to be made. The first is that we have no right to assume that because a letter is *signed* "K.H." it is necessarily *written* by KH. The use by a busy man of a secretary was, and still is, common practice. Sinnett and others stated expressly that KH frequently dictated his letters to pupils; and if these pupils learned English script from their master, a common similarity of outline is not surprising.\* The KH scripts preserved in the British Library are written in several very similar but nevertheless distinct hands.†

Secondly, in examining suspect letters or signatures, one does not pay much attention to the general outlines, since one can take it for granted that, unless a forgery is very crude, the outlines will be followed sufficiently well to be deceptive. It is the small unconscious mannerisms that are telling. Precisely because they are unconscious, they tend to persist for many years or even a lifetime; and they are difficult to eradicate. The fluency of the writing, and the variations in pressure that occur as the outlines are executed, can be all-important.‡

In the best of photocopies or photographic prints, much essential detail is lost from the original. All the stereoscopic detail goes; and some of the fine detail is confused or left unrecorded. Tonal values are distorted.§

THE PLATES IN THE HODGSON REPORT

The Hodgson Report includes two Plates which appear at first sight to be photographs of handwriting. It is important to realize that they are not. The groups of letters in Plate 1, which play a major part in Hodgson's argument, are (I quote) "copied from tracings of my own made from the original documents, and hence many of them exhibit a tremulous appearance which is not characteristic of the original MSS, and which might have been avoided if the work had been done entirely by the lithographic artist" (Hodgson Report, page 284). They are thus copies of copies. I find it hard to see the reason for this, since photography was well advanced in 1884 and photolithography from zinc plates had been in use for two decades. The reference to "lithographic artist" implies that the copies were drawn by hand directly on the plates by an artist who observed the material to be copied in a mirror and who used a pen charged with greasy ink — as was done in the early days of lithography. Mrs. Sidgwick in her Appendix XV (page 379) says: "The plates representing short passages from different documents give a good gen-

---

\*William Blake taught his wife to write; and her writing is almost indistinguishable from his.

†[This was my view at the time of writing, but see Opinion (5), p. 67. — V.H.]

‡[See Part 2, Methods of Examination, pp. 38-40. — V.H.]

§[Photocopies have much improved in quality during the past decade, but examination of the originals should always be made whenever possible. — V.H.]

eral idea of the writing, but in some instances fail in giving the individual character of particular letters. Still they are quite sufficiently accurate to help the reader to understand the discussion. Those copied from writing in blue pencil are, as might be expected, less close facsimiles than the others."

We have only assurances from Hodgson and Mrs. Sidgwick that the plates are good representations of the originals and we cannot gauge how much distortion has been introduced during the process of copying. These Plates, however, are the *only* positive evidence that Hodgson adduces. He devotes many pages to a description of what he has found during his examination of documents while in India and elsewhere, but we have only his word for it.

## The Handwriting Experts

I next examine the extraordinary behavior of Hodgson and the handwriting experts. I start with Mr. J. D. B. Gribble of Madras. In his "Report of an Examination into the Blavatsky Correspondence, published in the *Christian College Magazine*" (Higginbotham & Co., Madras, 1884), pages 7–9, he describes the forged Hartmann letter in the following terms:

> The handwriting of this letter bears only a very faint resemblance to that of Dr. Hartmann. The letters are written in an up-and-down style, and are by no means dissimilar to those of the anonymous and pseudonymous letters which one so frequently receives in this country. In fact, the difference between the handwriting of this document and that of Dr. Hartmann is so striking that one of two suppositions is at once forced upon the mind:—
> 
> (1) Either the person who wrote this letter had never seen, or had no opportunity of copying, Dr. Hartmann's handwriting;
> 
> (2) or else the person writing it *intended* that the receiver should at once detect the forgery.
> 
> The only instance in which any resemblance to Dr. Hartmann's writing is to be found is in the formation of the capital H. This, however, is very laboured and very forced.

Gribble states that he has examined this letter very carefully, and adds:

> That the Hartmann letter is so clumsy a forgery that its falseness would at once be apparent to any one who was acquainted with that gentleman's handwriting.

Thus Gribble. Hear now what Hodgson has to say about this self-same letter:

> The imitation of Dr. Hartmann's characteristics is for the most part exceedingly close, and on this point I must differ entirely from Mr. Gribble, who was evidently unfamiliar with Dr. Hartmann's writing; . . . . I should say that Mr. Gribble had the opportunity of examining the document only very hastily during a short visit of an hour at the headquarters of the Theosophical Society, when he examined other documents also; and this accounts for the mistakes which he made in his examination of it.

The contradiction here is absolute, and goes far beyond what one could reasonably attribute to faulty observation or general ineptitude. There is no way of reconciling the two statements. Had Hodgson given a facsimile of the Hartmann letter, we might have been able to decide whose description was correct; but no facsimile is given.

Netherclift and Sims were called upon to examine some of the KH documents. They both reached the conclusion that these documents were NOT written by Madame Blavatsky. This also was Gribble's opinion. Hodgson would have none of this, and says (page 282):

> I had already expressed my own conclusion, reached after an investigation of K.H. writings in India, that those I had examined were, with the exception of the K.H.(Y), written by Madame Blavatsky, and on my arrival in England I was surprised to find that Mr. Netherclift was of a different opinion concerning the K.H. writings submitted to him.

The final report was held up while more specimens were obtained, and (I quote):

> The result was that Mr. Netherclift came to the conclusion that the whole of these documents were without doubt written by Madame Blavatsky.

Mr. Sims of the British Museum changed his opinion to suit.

I find that the most revealing passage comes from Hodgson's own account (pages 296–7):

> My own view is that Mr. Damodar unquestionably wrote the K.H.(Z) as well as the K.H.(Y). Mr. Netherclift has had no opportunity of seeing the K.H.(Y), which was only lent to me for a short time in India, but the K.H.(Z) was submitted to him with the other K.H. documents upon which he was asked to give a second opinion, with the additional light afforded by those lent to us by Mr. Sinnett. Mr. Netherclift, in his second report, stated

as his opinion that it was "quite impossible that Damodar could have accommodated his usual style to suit that of K.H.," ... I then submitted to him my analysis of the document, and he kindly undertook to make a further examination, expressing his confidence that he would prove to me that the conclusion which I had reached was erroneous. The result, however, of a prolonged comparison which he then made was that he frankly confessed that my view was the correct one, saying that in the whole course of his many years' experience as an expert, he had "never met a more puzzling case," but that he was at last "thoroughly convinced that" the K.H.(Z) "was written by Damodar in *close imitation* of the style adopted by Madame Blavatsky in the K.H. papers." — pp. 296-7

Speaking as a professional examiner of questioned documents who has on occasion to undergo cross-examination in Court, I do not claim to be infallible. I give an opinion, and the reasons for that opinion, backed up by photographic and micrographic evidence wherever applicable. For legal purposes an opinion once given must stand. If a client does not agree with my findings, he is at liberty to go elsewhere and get further opinions. What I am not prepared to countenance is to have my client openly seeking to influence my judgment and, in effect, dictating what my report should be. I find Hodgson's blatant, and successful, efforts to influence the judgment of his experts highly improper. No English Court would accept a report known to have been made in such circumstances.

### Three Cardinal Statements

I now go to the heart of Hodgson's argument. He makes three cardinal statements (p. 283):

> I. That there are clear signs of development in the K.H. writing, various strong resemblances to Madame Blavatsky's ordinary handwriting having been gradually eliminated.
> II. That special forms of letters proper to Madame Blavatsky's ordinary writing, and not proper to the K.H. writing, occasionally appear in the latter.
> III. That there are certain very marked peculiarities of Madame Blavatsky's ordinary writing which occur throughout the K.H. writing.

I concentrate on the first and third, since, if these are wrong, the second has no importance.

*J'Accuse* / 17

First Cardinal Statement

Hodgson bases his thesis mainly on a series of KH letters lent by Mr. Sinnett, and he remarks:

> Facsimiles of the series of K.H. letters lent by Mr. Sinnett would perhaps have been interesting and suggestive to the reader,* and would have clearly shown the development of the K.H. hand; but Mr. Sinnett strongly emphasized his desire that no use whatever should be made of the specimens he submitted except for comparison of handwriting, and the facsimile production of portions of the documents was, of course, impossible without the publication, to some extent, of their substance. I have therefore chosen several small letters, *f*, *g*, *k* and *y*, for the purpose of illustrating the development I have mentioned. — pp. 283-4

To this I retort that it is easily possible to photograph portions of a document to show the characteristics of handwriting without revealing anything of the document's contents, and it is interesting to speculate why Hodgson did not do so.

Figures 1a and 1b are reproduced photographically from the Hodgson Report and show the development claimed for the *f* and *g*. Similar series are given by Hodgson for the letters *k* and *y*, but here the development is less striking.

Hodgson points out that HPB's ordinary *f*'s are commonly looped only below, and are usually preceded by an up stroke. The developed KH forms are looped only above. K.H. No. 1 and K.H. No. 2 show intermediate forms. Similar remarks apply to the *g*'s. This is the only *verifiable* evidence that Hodgson adduces in support of his statement. We examine the series more closely.

The row marked "B" is taken from the undoubted writings of Madame Blavatsky. Mr. Sinnett describes the others as follows:

> "No. 1 * * * is the first sheet of the first letter I ever had from him certainly through another hand.†
> 
> "Nos. 2 and 3 are selections from later letters of the old series written before publication of 'The Occult World.'
> 
> "No. 4 was received by me in London about the time 'Esoteric Buddhism' was published.
> 
> "No. 5 * * is from a letter certainly in K.H.'s own handwriting."

---
*They would indeed. — V.H.
†[A photograph of the whole page is reproduced in Figure 12. — V.H.]

We see therefore that Sinnett states explicitly that No. 1 is *from* KH but is *not written* by him. The date is about October 1880. The dates of Nos. 2 and 3 would be before June 1881. The date of No. 4 would be before June 1883. Sinnett affirms that No. 5 is in KH's own handwriting, but does not give the date.

This, forsooth, is a series selected for demonstrating the progressive development of the selfsame hand over a period of four years. We note that what Hodgson has shown us are isolated characters torn from their context. If we believe Sinnett, they are not all by the same writer. They are copies of copies. We do not know whether the letters selected are a fair sample taken from the manuscript or whether they have been specially selected to support Hodgson's case. We are told nothing of the other twenty-two letters of the alphabet.

What Hodgson does not mention is that his Plate 2 also covers a series of KH documents over the same period. The dates are:

| | |
|---|---|
| K.H.(i) | 1 November 1880* |
| K.H.(ii) to (vi) | 1881–1882 |
| K.H.(vii) | 1884 |

We are thus entitled to expect that *this* series should show a similar development of style. It shows nothing of the sort. K.H.(i) is fully "developed" and Figure 2 reproduces part of it directly from the Hodgson Report. Eight $f$'s are shown, all of which are looped above in a manner agreeing perfectly with K.H. No. 5 of Figure 1a. The same remarks apply to the $g$'s.

Either Hodgson did not notice that the evidence in his Plate 2 flatly contradicts his argument, or he elected to ignore it, concentrating on examples carefully selected to support his case. So much for his impartiality.

Many of the KH letters are preserved in the British Library, and I find from examination of these that fully "developed" KH writing, conforming in every respect to later KH letters, was being received as early as 29 October 1880. Other letters were written in writing very similar to, but nevertheless distinct from, KH's writing; and these may have been written by scribes.

There is no evidence for the "development" in the KH writing that Hodgson claims.

---

*[Referred to in detail in Part 2, p. 50. — V.H.]

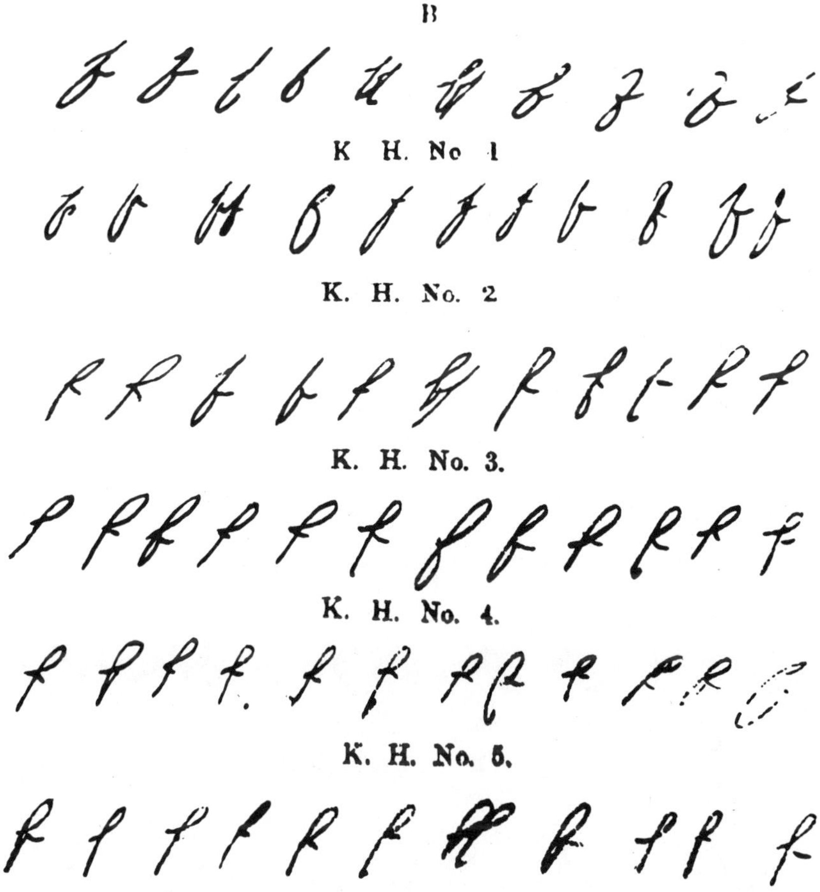

B

K. H. No 1

K. H. No. 2

K. H. No. 3.

K. H. No. 4.

K. H. No. 5.

FIGURE 1a.

THIRD CARDINAL STATEMENT

I quote Hodgson:

The evidence which we are now to consider is, in my view, the most important of all in proof of the fact* that the K.H. writings in general are the handiwork of Madame Blavatsky. This evidence depends on Madame Blavatsky's formation of the group of letters *a*, *d*, *g*, *o*, and *q*. The peculiarities exhibited in these letters are very striking; they are sufficiently shown in the specimens of *a*, *d*, *o*, and *q*, which I have given in group B"

───────────

*It was not a fact that the KH writings were the work of Madame Blavatsky; it was only Hodgson's hypothesis that this was so. — V.H.

20 / *H. P. Blavatsky and the SPR*

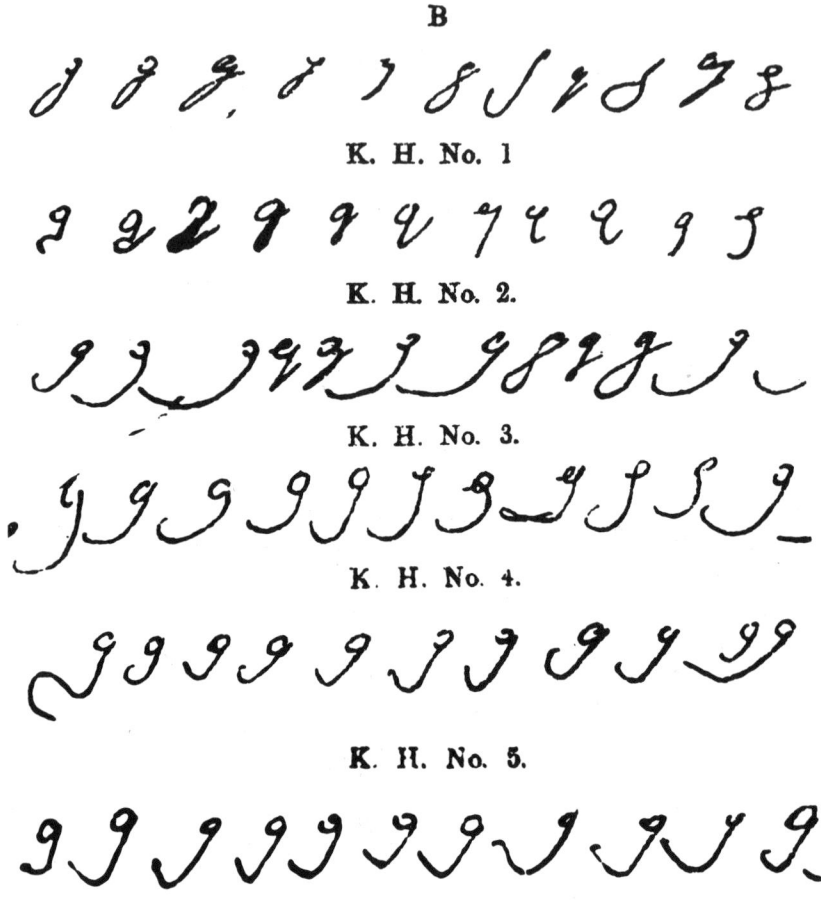

Figure 1b.

(all the letters in which are taken from the undoubted writings of Madame Blavatsky), and are apparent also in the different groups of *g*'s which I have given as manifesting the evolution of the characteristic K.H. *g*.

The group of B″ letters is reproduced from Hodgson in Figure 3, and the *g*'s are reproduced in line B of Figure 1b. Hodgson continues:

> A properly made "*o*" formation is uncommon both in Madame Blavatsky's ordinary handwriting and in the K.H. writings. If the letter requiring such a formation is initial, or not connected with the preceding letter, the tendency in both handwritings is to produce a formation akin to those shown in the first four *a*'s, the first three English *d*'s, and the first four *q*'s. If the letter is connected with the preceding letter, the tendency is either to begin

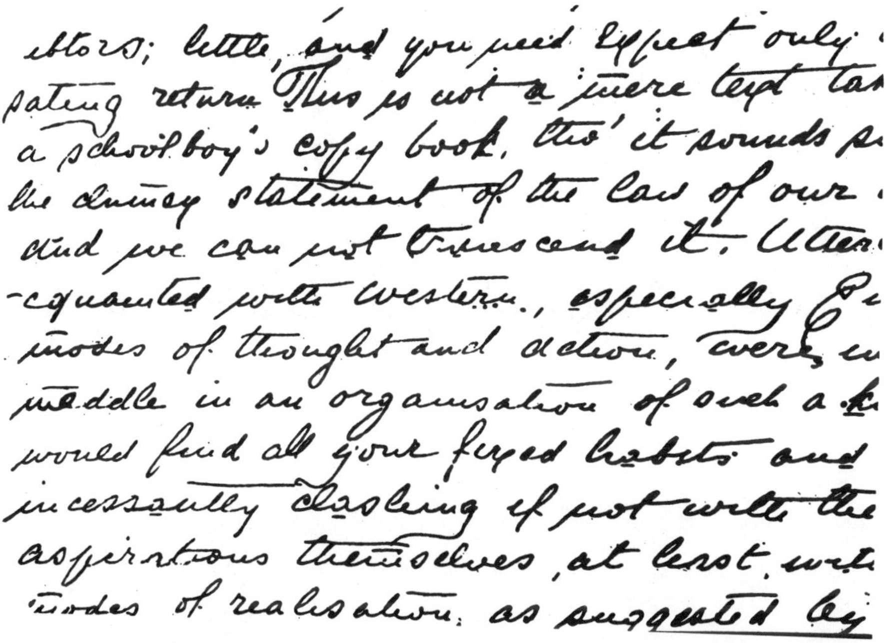

itors; little, and you need expect only
sating return. This is not a mere text to
a schoolboy's copy book, tho' it sounds p..
the clumsy statement of the law of our
and we can not transcend it. Utter..
-cquainted with Western., especially E..
modes of thought and action, were in
meddle in an organisation of such a k..
would find all your fixed habits and
incessantly clashing if not with the
aspirations themselves, at least with
modes of realisation. as suggested by

FIGURE 2.

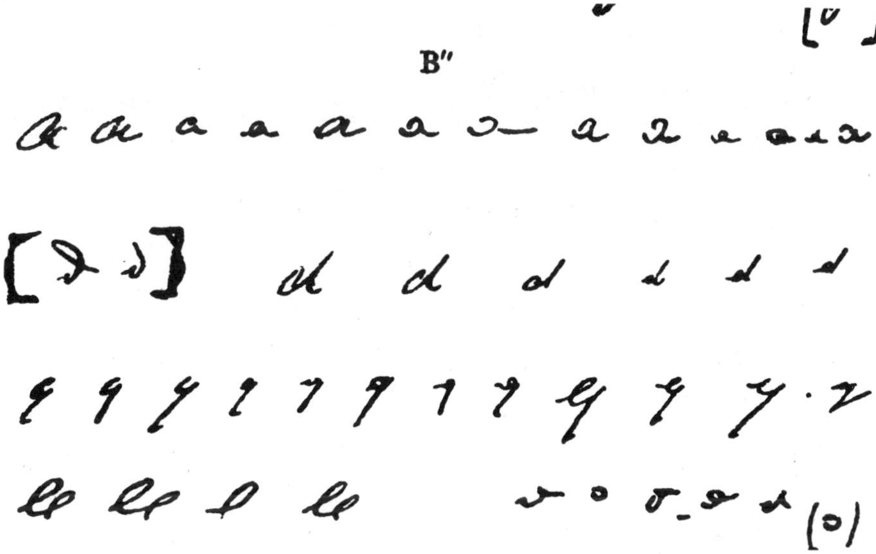

FIGURE 3.

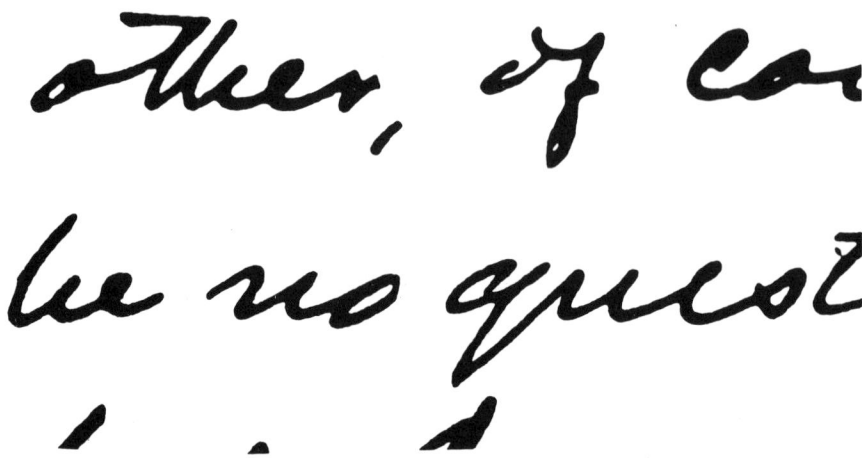

FIGURE 4a.

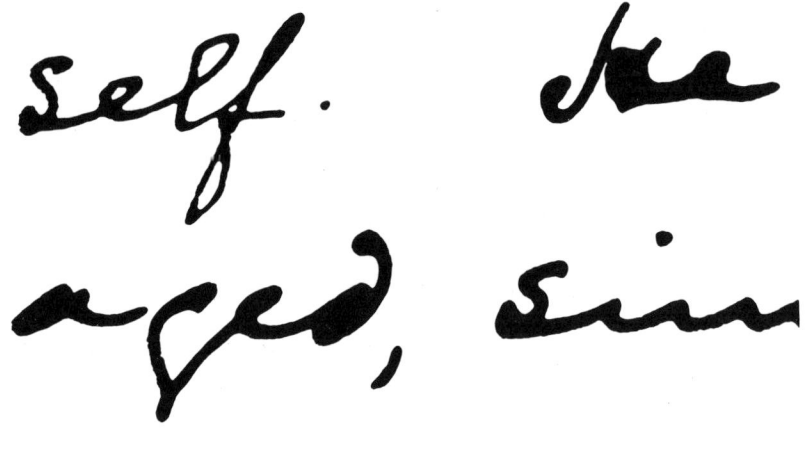

FIGURE 4b.

the "*o*" formation high up with a loop, as happens most commonly in the case of the *d*, leaving a gap above, — or to begin it low down, in which case the curve is rarely closed by a complete backward stroke, — and a peculiar gap therefore remains on the left-hand side. This last method of formation, which I shall call the *left-gap stroke*, may be clearly seen in some of the *q*'s and *o*'s, and is yet more noticeable in the *g*'s and *a*'s, of which last especially *it is the common, conspicuous, and most highly characteristic feature, both in Madame Blavatsky's ordinary writing and in those K.H. writings which I*

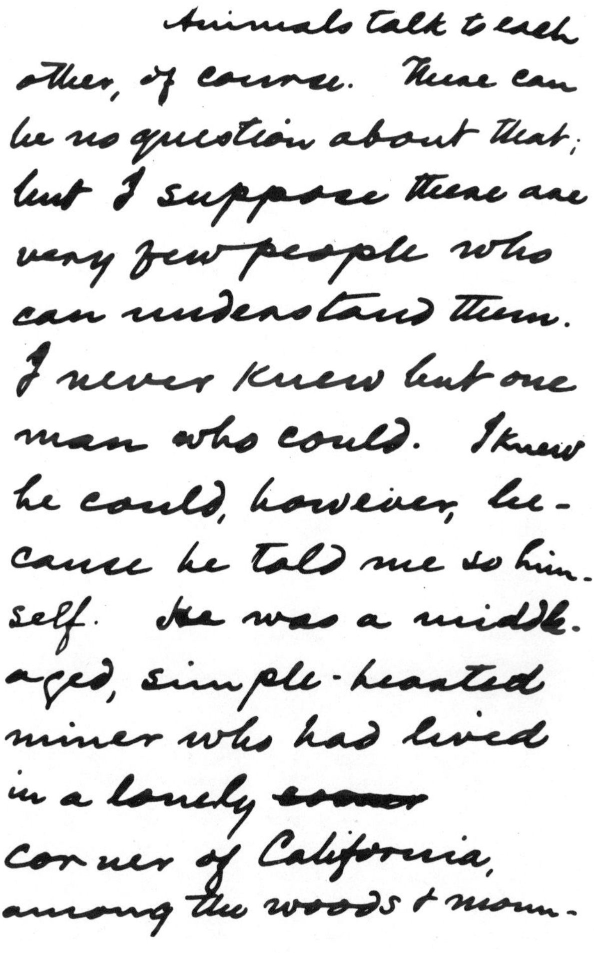

> Animals talk to each other, of course. There can be no question about that; but I suppose there are very few people who can understand them. I never knew but one man who could. I knew he could, however, because he told me so himself. He was a middle-aged, simple-hearted miner who had lived in a lonely corner of California, among the woods & mountains—

FIGURE 5.

*attribute to her.* It is so peculiar, that were it found but rarely in both sets of writings, or commonly in one and rarely in the other, it would still be a tolerably definite indication of identity of handiwork; but when we find, as we do, that it occurs constantly in both sets of writings, that any other form (except the *initial* forms spoken of) is comparatively rare, and that numerous varieties of the type in the one set of writings can be exactly paralleled in the other, there can, I think, be little doubt that one and the same person wielded the pen throughout.

Hodgson concludes the paragraph by saying:

> It must be difficult for any person to trace this *left-gap stroke* throughout a series of Madame Blavatsky's acknowledged writings, and throughout a set of what I believe to be her K.H. writings, comparing in detail all the swirling tricks and fantastic freaks of curvature which it adopts, and at the same time resist the impression that the same person executed them all.

The points made are well shown in Figures 4a and 4b, which should be compared with Figure 3 and Figure 1b. In Figure 4a, the *o* of "of" closely matches the *o* in the fourth line of Figure 3, fifth character from the left. It is followed by the typical Blavatskian *f*. The *o* in "other" can be seen in the fourth row, seventh character from the left, in the same Figure. The *q* in the second line of Figure 4a closely matches the *q* in Figure 3, third row, ninth character from the left. In the second line of Figure 4b, the word "aged" shows all the Blavatskian characteristics. The *a* can be found in Figure 3, row one, third character from the left. Madame Blavatsky makes a weird assortment of *g*'s, but the one in

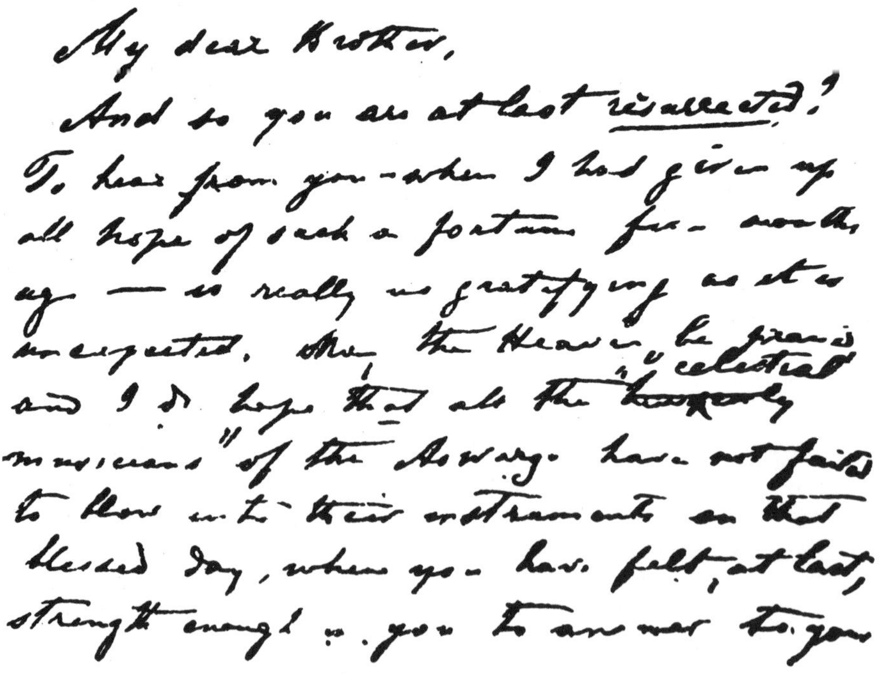
B (I.)

My dear Brother,
And so you are at last resurrected?
To hear from you—when I had given up all hope of such a fortune for months ago—is really as gratifying as it is unexpected. Thus the Heavens be praised and I do hope that all the ~~heavenly~~ celestial "musicians" of the Sowarga have not failed to blow into their instruments on that blessed day, when you have felt, at last, strength enough in you to answer to your

FIGURE 6.

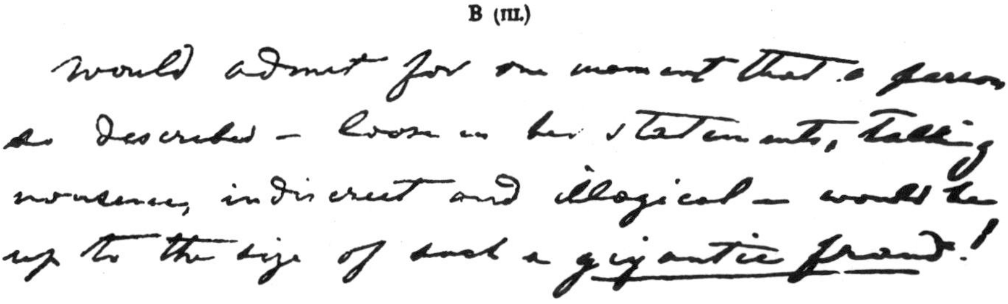

B (III.)

*would admit for one moment that a person as described — loose in her statements, talking nonsense, indiscreet and illogical — would be up to the size of such a gigantic fraud!*

FIGURE 7.

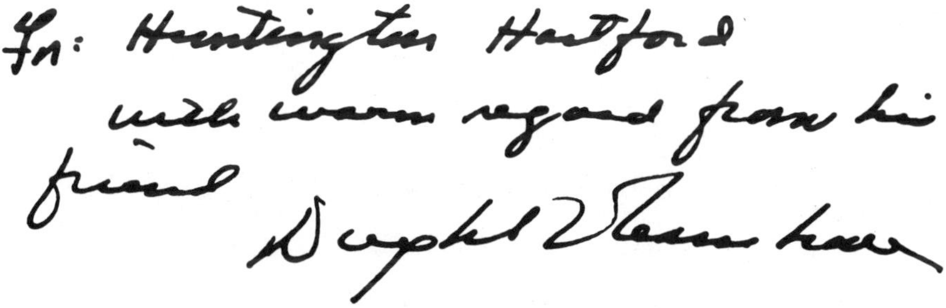

*To: Huntington Hartford with warm regard from his friend Dwight Eisenhower*

FIGURE 8.

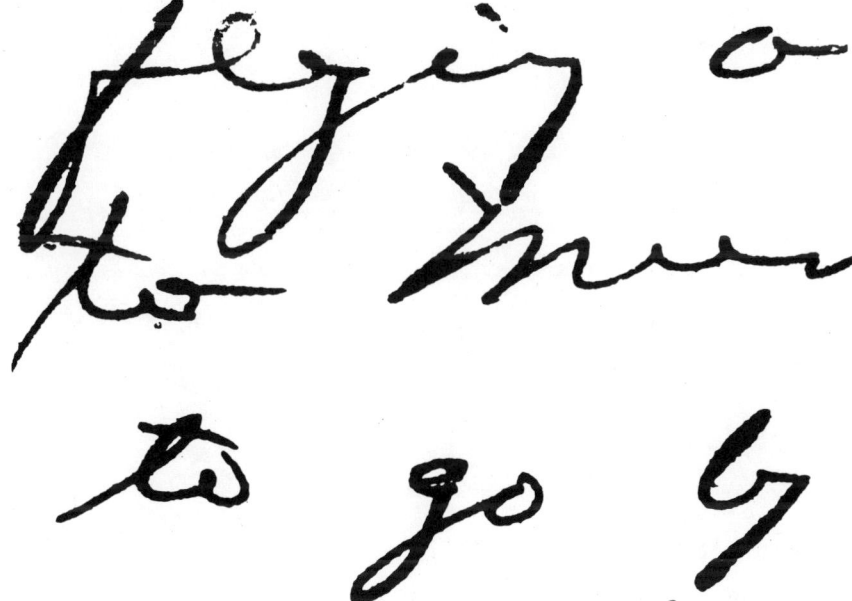

FIGURE 9.

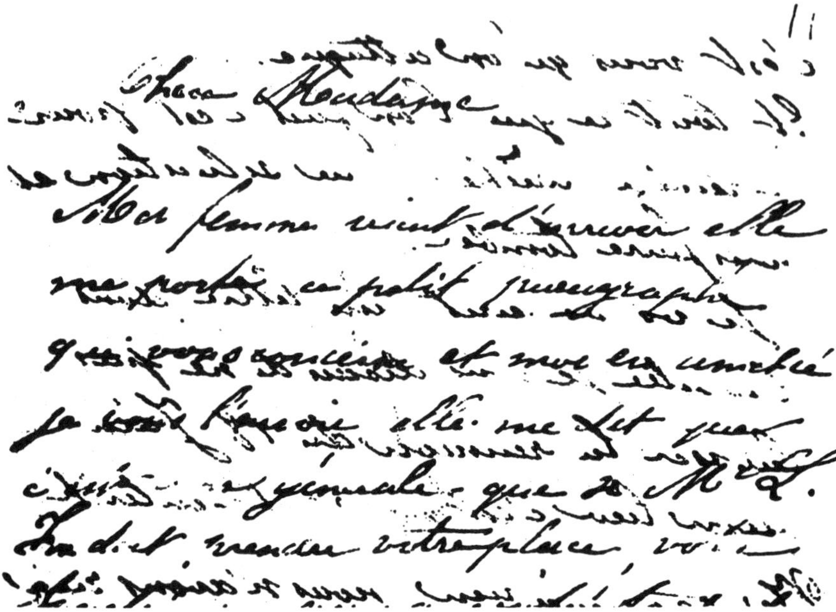

FIGURE 10a.

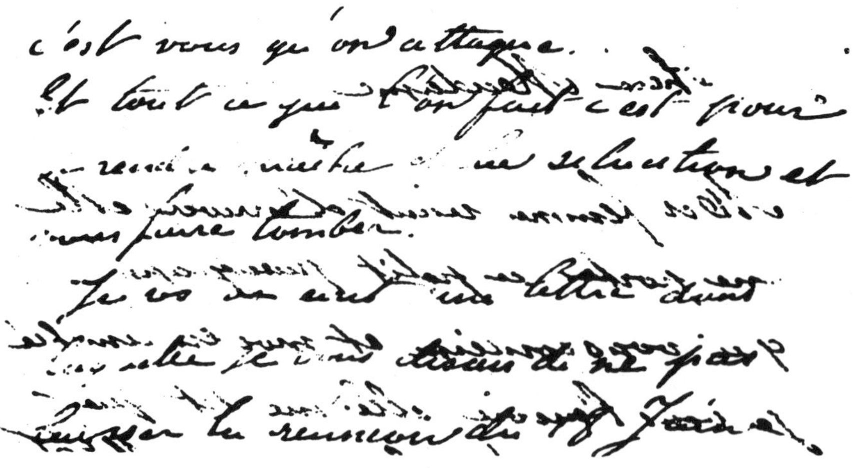

FIGURE 10b.

Figure 4b is clearly intermediate between the sixth and eighth characters from the left in the top line of Figure 1b. The *d* matches the second character from the left in row two of Figure 3.

It happens that the fragments of writing represented in Figures 4a and 4b were written, not by Madame Blavatsky, but by MARK TWAIN; and this will surely demonstrate the futility of trying to draw valid conclusions from an examination of letters torn from their context. The piece of writing to which 4a and 4b belong is reproduced in Figure 5, which is of interest because it shows that, like Madame Blavatsky, Mark Twain uses what Hodgson calls the German and English types of *d* indiscriminately. To be sure, Mark Twain's writing is not the same as HPB's, but it contains so many Blavatskian features that, using Hodgson's methods, one could prove that HPB wrote *Huckleberry Finn*.

Figures 6 and 7 reproduce two of the facsimiles of HPB's acknowledged writing given in Plate 1 of the Hodgson Report. Compare with them the writing shown in Figure 8. The slope is the same. The spacing is the same. The rhythm is the same. The formation of the important letters *f*, *g*, *h*, *m*, *n*, and *t* is, as near as may be, the same. The *a* of "regard" in line two of Figure 8 is a good specimen of Blavatskian left-gapping. However, the lines in Figure 8 were written, not by Madame Blavatsky, but by PRESIDENT EISENHOWER. The resemblance of his writing to HPB's is truly extraordinary. Through the courtesy of Ambassador John S. D. Eisenhower, I have been able to examine one of the late President's personal letters, written in the field about the close of World War II. Figure 9 shows a small enlarged portion. Note the beautiful examples of the *left-gap stroke*. Using Hodgson's methods, I could prove "without doubt" that *The Secret Doctrine* was written by Dwight D. Eisenhower.

Finally, I am much obliged to Mr. Michael Gomes for a photocopy of the *only* letter he has come across from the Coulombs in the Theosophical Society archives at Adyar. It is from Mr. Coulomb, imploring HPB not to eject him from the Bungalow and saying that they can explain all when she arrives. Being on thin paper, the writing shows through to the reverse side; and both sides are recorded in the photocopy as shown in Figures 10a and 10b. Nevertheless, some of the writing is plain enough. Figure 10a starts:

> Chère Madame
> Ma femme vient d'arriver elle me porte un petit paragraphe qui vous concerne et moi en amitié je vous l'envoie elle me dit . . .

Figure 10b starts:

> C'est vous qu'on attaque
> Et tout ce que l'on fait c'est pour se rendre maître de la situation et vous faire tomber . . .

Note the remarkable left-gappery in the

> q of "qui" on line 4 of Figure 10a
> qu in line 1, Figure 10b, and
> que in line 2 of Figure 10b

and compare with them the *q*'s of Figure 3.

Note also the construction of the *a*'s in

> amitié in line 4 of Figure 10a
> attaque in line 1 of Figure 10b, and
> situation in line 3 of Figure 10b

and compare with them the *a*'s of Figure 3.

These examples surely suffice to show that there is nothing uniquely characteristic about the letters represented in Figure 3 and the first line of Figure 1b. The presence of the *left-gap stroke* does not prove that the writer was H. P. Blavatsky.

Hodgson's Third Cardinal Statement is false.

What Figures 10a and 10b do show is that Coulomb, having close acquaintance with and access to HPB's writing, and also the initial advantage of having writing similar to hers in important respects, could have interpolated passages into her genuine letters without much difficulty.* Why did Hodgson not even consider this possibility? Why were no specimens of Mr. Coulomb's writing sent for independent examination?

Gribble, in his "Report," says that if Madame Blavatsky did not write the incriminating correspondence, the only other suspects are the Coulombs. (Granted; they had ample motive.) He states that Madame Coulomb's writing was quite unlike that of Madame Blavatsky. (This is as may be.) However, he goes on to dismiss Mr. Coulomb in the extraordinary statement:

---

*[See Part 2, p. 43, 2nd paragraph. — V.H.]

Mr. Coulomb may at once be relieved from any suspicion. He is only imperfectly acquainted with English, and it would have been an impossibility for him to have written the letters.

One is constrained to ask, in the name of Heaven, why? Most of the incriminating passages were written, not in English, but in French — and bad French to boot. A forger has to have a keen eye and memory for outlines, and skill in controlling a pen; he does not have to compose the matter he is forging. Madame Coulomb could have done that for him.

## What Hodgson Does Not Mention

It is hardly a surprise now to find that there are systematic differences between the writing in the KH scripts and HPB's acknowledged writing which Hodgson does not mention. I take three of the more important letters.

The "developed" KH scripts (which, as I have said, start as early as October 1880) show a remarkable formation of the letter *p*: the main down stroke and the return up stroke are widely separated, and the final loop is degenerate. Examples showing clearly what I mean will be found in Figure 2:

in line 1 — "expect"
in line 3 — "copy"
in line 6 — "especially," and
in line 11 — "aspirations."

With HPB, the main down stroke and the return up stroke usually overlap in the normal manner. Examples will be seen in

Figure 6, line 4 — "hope"
Figure 6, line 6 — "unexpected" and "praised"
Figure 6, line 7 — "hope"
Figure 7, line 1 — "person" and
Figure 7, line 4 — "up."

The difference is persistent and significant.

*h*. In the KH scripts the leading stroke and main down stroke of the letter *h* are made in a continuous movement, and the down stroke is concave to the right. The final "hump" is low and strongly skew to the right. Good examples are shown in

>Figure 2, line 3 — "tho"
>Figure 2, line 7 — "thought"
>Figure 2, line 9 — "habits," and
>Figure 2, line 10 — "clashing."

The *h* in HPB's writing has a down stroke that is either straight or slightly concave to the left, and the "hump" is much less skew. Examples are shown in

>Figure 6, line 3 — "hear," "when," "had"
>Figure 6, line 4 — "hope"
>Figure 6, line 7 — "hope," "that"
>Figure 6, line 8 — "have."

The difference is persistent and significant.

*n* and *m*. The initial *n* in the KH scripts is usually like the Greek letter "mu" with a long leading stroke. Examples are:

>Figure 2, line 1 — "need"
>Figure 2, line 5 — "not"
>Figure 2, line 10 — "not."

Within a word there is little difference between *n* and *u*. The letter *m* exhibits the same peculiarities. Examples are:

>Figure 2, line 2 — "mere"
>Figure 2, line 7 — "modes"
>Figure 2, line 8 — "meddle"
>Figure 2, line 12 — "modes"

HPB's *m*'s and *n*'s follow a saw-tooth pattern, the up strokes being at roughly 30° and the down strokes at about 80° to the horizontal. Examples are shown in

>Figure 6, line 8 — "musicians," "not"
>Figure 7, line 1 — "moment"
>Figure 7, line 3 — "nonsense"

The difference is persistent and significant.

   I do not think it is necessary to proceed further. If HPB wrote the Mahatma Letters, she did not gradually perfect her style, as Hodgson maintains. She had to get it right, from the beginning. Every time she made an *f*, a *g*, an *h*, a *p*, an *n*, or an *m*, she had to remember to make the right outlines while maintaining fluency and avoiding any reversion to her normal style. The KH documents that I have examined in the British Library are fluent in their execution and show no sign of hesitancy. I can find no clear evidence that HPB wrote them and I find significant evidence that she did not. I do not know who wrote the Mahatma Letters, but I do not find it plausible to assume that Madame Blavatsky wrote them — the great bulk of them at any rate.

That is my professional Opinion.

### The Writing on the Letters

The Mahatma Letters show several curious features. I am not saying that they are paranormal, but they at least excite interest. In general, the documents appear to be written either in black ink, or in blue or red pencil, on any piece of paper that happened to be available. I say, "appear to be written," because I would like laboratory confirmation that the black marks *are* composed of the writing ink of the period; and I would like to know the composition of the pencils — if pencils were used.

I take first those documents apparently written in colored pencil. On many, though not all, the writing is built up, not of normal pencil strokes, but of thin parallel lines, spaced at about forty to the inch and inclined at about thirty degrees to the horizontal. This goes on for page after page with the greatest regularity. The lines are sharply defined, and the spaces between them are either devoid of color, or are filled by a uniform pale blue or pink tint. When the spaces between the lines are clear, the writing looks as if it had been made with a modern ink-jet printer coupled to an electronic scanner.*

Something like this effect can be produced by writing with the paper supported on ribbed bookcloth; and Madame Coulomb affirmed that this is how the writing was done. Why one should want to use so uncomfortable a support for no apparent reason is not explained.

I have a large collection of artists' colored pencils in four different makes, besides Conté crayon, carbon, graphite and chinagraph pencils. I have experimented with a selection of these on various papers supported on ribbed covers of books taken from my library, and I cannot get the clean, sharp effect shown by many of the Mahatma pencil scripts. Signs of pencil drag, pencil debris between the lines, and irregularity of outline and line spacing are always apparent. This is not to say that the

---

*[See Figure 11 in color plates (facing p. 48). The extreme regularity of the striations may be checked by draftsmen's parallel rulers and a protractor. — V.H.]

effect cannot be reproduced; it is to say that, so far, I have not been able to do so, despite some effort.

The documents that appear to be written in black ink are equally fascinating. The dark marks seem to be within the paper rather than on the surface. It is hard to be sure of this now, because the bound letters have been laminated in archival tissue in order to preserve them. One has therefore, to distinguish between the fibers of the protective tissue and the fibers of the paper of the letter itself.

What is certain is that corrections have been made to the text *with great care*, by erasing words or whole phrases, and writing the corrections over the erasure. These erasures have not been made by rubbing with a hard rubber or by scraping with a knife, for there is no local weakening of the paper. It seems that a chemical ink eradicator has been used; but application of liquid reagents usually disturbs the surface fibers of paper and leaves faint stains that are hard to eradicate. Signs of this are not obvious. It would be interesting to know from laboratory tests whether there are traces of chemical residues in the paper in these regions; if there are not, it may be that the corrections were made on originals of which the documents now preserved in the British Library are copies.

It is impossible to answer these questions under the conditions of the Reading Room, armed only with a pocket microscope. One can only hope that one day permission will be given for the necessary (non-destructive) laboratory work to be done.

Conclusion

I have concentrated on the handwriting aspect of the Hodgson Report, partly because it forms a major part of his thesis and I am here playing on my home ground, but more importantly because everything I have stated can be checked independently. We do not have to rely on the testimony of long-dead witnesses. The witness here — and an eloquent one — is the Hodgson Report itself.

As detailed examination of this Report proceeds, one becomes more and more aware that, whereas Hodgson was prepared to use any evidence, however trivial or questionable, to implicate HPB, he ignored all evidence that could be used in her favor. His report is riddled with slanted statements, conjecture advanced as fact or probable fact, uncorroborated testimony of unnamed witnesses, selection of evidence and downright falsity.

As an investigator, Hodgson is weighed in the balances and found wanting. His case against Madame H. P. Blavatsky is not proven.

I cannot exonerate the SPR committee from blame for publishing this thoroughly bad report. They seem to have done little more than rubber-stamp Hodgson's opinions; and no serious attempt was made to check his findings or even to read his report critically. If they had done so, its errors of procedure, its inconsistencies, its faulty reasoning and bias, its hostility towards the subject and its contempt for the "native" and other witnesses, would have become apparent; and the case would have been referred back for further study. Madame H. P. Blavatsky was the most important occultist ever to appear before the SPR for investigation; and never was opportunity so wasted.

Nor can I exonerate the quondam Council of the Theosophical Society for their failure to allow their founder fair defense. They seemed concerned only with saving their own reputations. Whether she was impostor or not, HPB was entitled to a fair hearing. She never had it. Had she been allowed the legal and expert help she begged for, both Hodgson and the Society for Psychical Research would have been in dire trouble.

It is a thing most wonderful that Hodgson was able so completely to bamboozle, not only Netherclift and Mr. Sims of the British Museum, but also men and women of the caliber of Myers, Gurney, and Mrs. Sidgwick — not to mention several generations of psychical researchers since the 1885 Report was published.

On 14 January 1886, Madame Blavatsky wrote:

> That Mr. Hodgson's elaborate but misdirected inquiries, his affected precision, which spends infinite patience over trifles and is blind to facts of importance, his contradictory reasoning and his manifold incapacity to deal with such problems as those he endeavoured to solve, will be exposed by other writers in due course — I make no doubt.
> — *H. P. Blavatsky: Collected Writings* 7:9

I apologize to her that it has taken us one hundred years to demonstrate that she wrote truly.

PART 2

# J'Accuse d'autant plus

A Further Study of the Hodgson Report

PART 2

# J'Accuse d'autant plus*

THE EXPERT WITNESS

I start this part by describing the work of the Expert Witness as it applies to English Courts, and with particular reference to Handwriting Experts.

The Expert Witness is there to assist the Court in cases where specialist knowledge of some subject is needed. He should *never* try to act as advocate, and his prime duty is always to the Court and not to the solicitor, person, or organization that has hired him. If he is hired by the Defense and finds that he has to give an opinion in favor of the Prosecution, then so be it. He should never change his mind under duress from his employer.

To be accepted in Court, reports from witnesses normally have to take the Statement of Witness form prescribed by Section 9 of the Criminal Justice Act of 1967. It starts with the declaration:

> This statement consisting of ___ pages each signed by me is true to the best of my knowledge and belief and I make it knowing that, if it is tendered in evidence, I shall be liable to prosecution if I have wilfully stated in it anything which I know to be false or do not believe to be true.

This declaration has to be signed, dated, and witnessed. After the declaration the report usually continues along the following lines.

There are two main parts to the report. Part A contains four sections. The first gives an outline of the Expert's qualifications for and experience of the job. He is liable to be questioned about this in Court. The second must give precise identification of the documents received for examination. For example, in a letter, this should give the date (if known), to whom and by whom the letter was written, and the opening and closing sentences. "A letter written on green paper" will not do.

---

*"I accuse all the more."

The third section should state the Expert's instructions — what exactly he was asked to do. He will normally keep within these instructions. The final section should state the Expert's Opinion, based on the evidence that he has been given, and an indication of the strength of that Opinion ranging from near certainty for or against through a neutral or "don't know" position.

An Opinion is a formal statement of reasons for a judgment given, a judgment which has often to be based on grounds short of proof. Here the statement should be as brief and clear as possible, leaving the detailed reasons to Part B of the report. An Opinion once given must stand unless new evidence comes to light which makes a revision necessary.

Part B of the report contains the detailed reasons for the Expert's Opinion, which he will have to defend in Court if the report is contested (as it often is). In this case, he will have to give his evidence in person and under oath. He must be prepared to withstand stringent cross-examination from "the other side" and, above all, he must keep his temper. Court hearings are highly adversarial, but usually without personal rancor. They are a far cry from academic discussions.

Sometimes the "Section 9" Statement of Witness is not enough, and the report has to be presented by Affidavit, drawn up by, and signed and sworn before, a solicitor, and neatly tied up with blue ribbon.

The Expert Witness should always remember that he is not describing what happens when sulphuric acid is poured onto zinc: he is helping to pass judgment on another human being whose life may be profoundly and permanently affected if his witness is careless, biased, or flawed. It is an awesome responsibility, particularly when the available evidence is meager or conflicting. I would that parapsychologists should remember that they may be in the same position.

I mention all this because it is evident that Hodgson, like Gallio,* cared for none of these things. I grant that Court procedure may have been less stringent than it is today (though I am not sure about this), but Hodgson's methods are inexcusably lax and would never stand up in Court now.

## Methods of Examination

Methods of examination differ in detail according to the examiner, but some basic principles are common to most.

---

*Acts 18:17.

First, there is the "feel" of the writing as a whole. Hodgson states:

> The little importance that can be attached to the mere general appearance of a written document is well enough known to persons who are at all familiar with the comparisons of handwritings. — p. 283

This is strongly denied by Charles Hamilton who does claim some experience in the examination of documents (*In Search of Shakespeare: A Study of the Poet's Life and Handwriting*, Robert Hale, London, 1986, pp. 7-8):

> The feel of handwriting is nothing more than the instantaneous impression it creates upon a practiced eye. Far from being an amorphous test of authenticity, feel is actually the sum total of the viewer's knowledge, the fusion of intuition and an immense amount of experience. After the manuscript expert has made a feel judgment, his split-second impression can be crystallized by a detailed examination of the script. . . .
> 
> Feel is the key factor in comparing scripts or in judging authenticity. The occasional examiner of questioned handwriting may be impervious to feel. He may study laboriously the formation of individual letters in a document. . . .
> 
> Some of the factors that contribute to the feel of a manuscript are: the amount of space between words and between lines; the size of the script; the ease, or lack of ease, with which the script flows; the pressure of the pen in forming strokes, especially descending strokes; the length of the descending strokes, as in *y*'s and *g*'s; the overall legibility of the script; the position of the dots over the *i*'s and the crossbars of the *t*'s; the thickness of the pen strokes; and the haste, or lack of haste, with which the words and letters have been formed. . . .
> 
> Once a manuscript passes the feel test, a thorough examination of individual words and letters is in order.

To Hamilton's list I should like to add: relative size of capitals to small letters; relative length of ascenders and descenders to the body of small letters; abnormal lateral compression or extension of words; style, detached or running; consistency and fluency.

If writing *looks* wrong, it probably *is* wrong; but detailed examination may be needed to establish *why* it is wrong. "Feel" comes only with experience.

After the "feel" test, the second stage of the examination begins where the script is viewed under magnification, word by word, letter by letter. One seeks to ascertain the methods of execution of individual letters, the order of the pen strokes and the pressure variations. Photomicrographs made at a magnification of around ×4 diameters are often informative and helpful. One should remember that differences are just as important as similarities, often more so.

Finally, there comes the search for significant idiosyncrasies, usually unconscious, which can help to make identification of a hand more certain. Such idiosyncrasies may be as small as the method of making the dot over the letter *i*. In my own handwriting, the loops to the letters *a*, *g*, *o*, and *q* are all made by a continuous *clockwise* movement of the pen. This is rare and not immediately obvious.

I conclude this section with a few important observations. It is often relatively easy to forge a signature freehand and from memory. It is much harder to write a single-page original letter in an assumed hand without reverting at some point to one's normal practice. It is harder still to write page after page of original composition in reply to specific questions in assumed handwriting *and* literary style, without reversions to normal practice. One or two of the KH letters top 16,000 words and they deal with abstruse subjects.

From an examiner's point of view, it is often quite easy to say that a piece of writing has been forged: it is more difficult by far to say *by whom* it was forged. To assert that one particular person was responsible, to the exclusion of all others, can be very risky.

Quite recently, in my own practice, I was asked to examine the handwriting of a threatening note which featured in a Crown Court case. As is usual with Crown Court documentary exhibits, the note was placed in a transparent envelope to which was attached an identification label. The details were filled in by the police officer who had questioned the witness who had provided the exhibit, and the witness had signed the label to authenticate it. I found, to my astonishment, that the police officer's handwriting was almost identical with the writing on the threatening note; but there was no likelihood that the police officer was responsible for the crime and the similarity of the writing was coincidental. It is quite wrong, and dangerous, to pick out one suspect to the exclusion of all others, and then search for evidence to incriminate that one suspect. That is what Hodgson did and I find his behavior inexcusable.

## The Hodgson Report

THE "PHENOMENA"

I have little to say about the first section (by far the longest) of the Hodgson Report. I have no means of telling whether or not any of the "phenomena" attributed to HPB were genuine. I was not there at the time; all the witnesses to the phenomena are long since dead; and all tangible evidence like the "Shrine" is lost or destroyed. The whole matter is shrouded in the mists of history and legend, and it seems unlikely now that any fresh evidence will come to light. The "phenomena" could have been performed by sleight of hand: whether they were so done, I am unable to say. I am therefore agnostic in the sense coined by T. H. Huxley: "I don't know." Fortunately, the enduring value of HPB's writing does not depend upon "phenomena."

This said, I do note Hodgson's hostility towards HPB and the contempt with which all but two of the witnesses are dismissed, often for ludicrous reasons.* The only two witnesses whose word Hodgson accepts without question are the Coulombs; and if they turn out to be untrustworthy, Hodgson's edifice collapses.

THE HANDWRITING

*The Blavatsky-Coulomb Letters*

These letters are of *crucial* importance, since if the incriminating portions of the letters are genuine, they show that HPB was involved in fraudulent practices. If, on the other hand, they were forgeries, in whole or in part, the only other suspects were the Coulombs; and the forgeries would mean that the Coulombs were lying and their evidence in other matters could not be trusted.

Since writing "J'Accuse," I have had the benefit of Michael Gomes'

---

*The first known letter from KH was delivered by a "mysterious stranger" about 1870 according to the testimony of Madame Fadeyef. This testimony is dismissed by Hodgson on the grounds that "we should remember that she is a Russian lady, and the aunt of Madame Blavatsky, and that Madame Blavatsky may have been influenced by political motives in the founding of the Theosophical Society." I think it possible that on occasion even Russian ladies can tell the truth. The quotation comes from page 292 of the Hodgson Report and the whole footnote deserves study as an example of Hodgson's reasoning.

painstaking research into the Coulomb affair* and of his valuable annotated bibliography,† of which Chapter 8 is particularly relevant to the present study. The work of Beatrice Hastings‡ on the Coulomb pamphlet§ is not readily available, but is essential reading.

Unfortunately it seems that these vitally important letters have been destroyed. What we do know of them can be summarized thus:

Some of the letters from HPB to Emma Coulomb (which must have been numerous) contained short passages purporting to be instructions to EC for producing fraudulent phenomena.

Very few Theosophists (not even HPB herself) were permitted to examine these letters. Maj. Gen. H. R. Morgan, who did inspect one referring to himself, declared it to be a forgery.¶

No facsimile of these letters was published by Hodgson, who gave the flimsiest of reasons for not doing so.

The key witness here is Netherclift, whose qualifications and background I have been unable to discover. His report, as published by Hodgson, is mutilated, part being excised, and it carries two dates. As stated, some of the documents Netherclift lists cannot be identified, and those that can be identified are not incriminating. Some are only envelopes. In his report, Hodgson "stars" some extracts from documents which he says he sent to Netherclift for examination, but it is hard to reconcile the "starring" with Netherclift's list.

A second batch of unidentified documents was sent to Netherclift, who returned them with an *endorsement on the envelope containing them* to the effect that they were all in the handwriting of HPB. The envelope could have contained HPB's laundry lists for all we know to the contrary.

---

*Michael Gomes, "The Coulomb Case 1884–1984," *The Theosophist*, December 1984, January 1985, February 1985, pp. 95-102, 138-47, 178-86.

†Michael Gomes, *Theosophy in the Nineteenth Century: An Annotated Bibliography*, Garland Reference Library of Social Sciences, Vol. 532 (Religious Information Systems Vol. 15), Garland Publishing, New York & London, 1994.

‡Beatrice Hastings, *Defence of Madame Blavatsky*, Vols. 1 & 2, The Hastings Press, Worthing, England, 1937.

§Emma Coulomb, *Some Account of My Intercourse with Madame Blavatsky from 1872–1884*, Higginbotham & Co., Madras, 1884.

¶*Reply by H. R. Morgan to a Report of an Examination of the Blavatsky Correspondence by J. D. B. Gribble*, Ootacamund, 1884.

I have some information about Mr. Sims of the British Museum.* He seems to have done little more than act as Tweedledee to Netherclift's Tweedledum. No written report from him is reproduced by Hodgson.

It seems that Hodgson never examined Alexis Coulomb's handwriting. It was very similar to HPB's.† At the time of writing "J'Accuse" I was not aware that this was well known to Theosophists. It is related that on at least one occasion Coulomb issued fraudulent instructions from HPB "as a joke."‡

The last known recipient of the letters was Elliott Coues who bought them for his defense in a lawsuit.§ If genuine, they would have provided damning evidence in his favor. He did not use them. HPB's death terminated the suit, but a year later the New York *Sun* published an editorial retraction.¶

The check for the letters is preserved in Coues' papers** but the letters themselves have not been found despite diligent search for them by Anita Atkins and others.††

After Coues' death, a quantity of Blavatsky correspondence was burnt by Coues' heir.‡‡

It is unlikely now that we shall ever be able to submit the incriminating portions of these letters to independent examination, but the circumstantial evidence that they were forgeries by Alexis Coulomb is strong. He had both motive and ability for so doing. I cannot believe that Coues would not have used the letters to harm HPB had they been genuine. Maybe Coues, realizing that they were useless to him, had them destroyed rather than that they should find their way into the Blavatsky camp.

---

*See Part 1, p. 9.
†See Part 1, pp. 27-8.
‡Sylvia Cranston, *HPB: The Extraordinary Life and Influence of Helena Blavatsky,* Jeremy P. Tarcher/Putnam, New York, 1993, p. 270.
§Michael Gomes, "Witness for the Prosecution: Annie Besant's Testimony on behalf of H. P. Blavatsky in the New York *Sun* / Coues Law Case," Occasional Paper, *Theosophical History,* Fullerton, CA, 1993.
¶ Text of the retraction is reproduced in Cranston, *HPB,* p. 377.
**Cranston, *HPB,* p. 271.
††Information from Anita Atkins. See Part 1, p. 7.
‡‡Information from Walter A. Carrithers. See Part 1, p. 8.

## The Mahatma Letters

Fortunately most of the Mahatma Letters are preserved in the British Library where they were deposited by Sinnett's executrix. They are available for study on request in the Department of Manuscripts (Additional MSS 45284, 45285, and 45286). THEY ARE PRIMARY EVIDENCE. There are, however, difficulties in the way of examining them in the British Library. The letters themselves are bound in three heavy and bulky volumes so that side-by-side comparison of different letters is often awkward or impossible. For valid reasons one is not allowed to use pen, pencil, or drawing instruments in the reading room. Photography is prohibited. Only the use of a hand lens is permitted. Even a midget pocket microscope of ×30 magnification was viewed askance by the library attendants and had to be put away discreetly in my pocket. For those who live outside the London area, work in the British Library can be both time-consuming and expensive.

Thanks to the Theosophical Society with International Headquarters at Pasadena, California, I have been lent for several years a valuable set of 1,323 color slides of the complete collection of the Mahatma Letters in the British Library, which I have been allowed to study in detail for as long as I thought necessary. I can now say much more about the Letters than was possible in "J'Accuse."

The text of the Letters has been published by Barker.* This includes letters, fragments, and endorsements from KH (108), M (26), HPB (9), Subba Row (3, one with added comments by KH), A. O. Hume (2), A. P. Sinnett (2), the "Disinherited" (1), Stainton Moses (1) and Damodar (1). The Letters are worth reading in their own right, but they can be hard to follow because subjects can be presented in no particular order and they can be answers to unrecorded questions. KH is inclined to be long-winded and discursive; and he can often start to answer one question and, before going far, veer off to answer another (unasked) question.

Viewing the slides was tedious and time-consuming. To get the required detail, each of the 1,323 slides was examined under a micro-

---

*A. Trevor Barker, ed., *The Mahatma Letters to A. P. Sinnett*, facsimile 2nd Edition (1926), Theosophical University Press, Pasadena, 1994; Third and Revised Edition, The Theosophical Publishing House, Adyar, Madras, 1962.

scope at ×50 magnification, using the mechanical stage of the microscope to scan the text line by line. After an hour of this, one had to have a break.

*The Paper* used for the Letters seems to have been any scrap that came to hand. According to KH, paper was a scarce commodity and all available pieces were used, even parts left blank by a previous correspondent. Some of the paper was of "rice paper" thickness.

*The Ink* presents some problems. It has not faded in the manner of the ordinary writing inks of the period, which in the course of a century fade through brown and yellow to complete invisibility. These have remained legible and look as if they were confined to a thin layer on the surface of the paper. There is little "strike through." This is a term used by printers to denote penetration of ink through the pores of the paper to the reverse side. Victorian writing inks used to penetrate right through thin paper and make writing on the reverse side impossible (see Part 1, Figures 10a and 10b).

Negotiations with the Trustees of the Letters to have these inks tested nondestructively by a university for their chemical composition led nowhere; and now that the papers have been strengthened by enclosure in archival tissue, further research on this problem may prove impossible.

*Blue Pencil*: a knotty problem is the writing which appears to be in blue pencil or crayon. Much of this writing (but not all) has a clean, sharp, striated structure reminiscent of a mackerel sky. It looks as if it had been made by a modern, precision line scanner (see Figure 11). To me, the reason for this method of production remains a mystery. Emma Coulomb is reported to have said that the effect was made by writing with the paper resting upon bookcloth. I cannot understand why anyone should want to write with the paper resting on bookcloth; in any case, I cannot get the effect by writing in this way. The irregularities of the bookcloth and the dragging of pigment into the strips which should remain clear are immediately apparent. This remarkable feature of the writing has been ignored by most of the writers on the subject of the Mahatma Letters whom I have come across.

*Corrections*: A further feature of the KH Letters is that corrections have been made to the text with much care. These corrections often entail the erasure of whole words, or even of whole phrases, and writing the corrections over the erasure. The erasures have not been made by rubbing with a hard rubber or by scraping with a knife, for there is no local weakening of the paper. It looks as if a chemical ink eradicator has been used; but application of liquid reagents usually disturbs the surface fibers of the paper and leaves faint stains that are hard to remove. It would be useful to know from laboratory tests whether there are traces of chemical residues in these places. If there are not, it may be that the corrections were made on *originals*, of which the Letters preserved in the British Library are copies. Knowing nothing of the method of transmission of these Letters, I do not know whether this suggestion is plausible.

The history of these Letters and abundant references have been given by Gomes.* The last letter believed to have come from KH was received in 1900 by Annie Besant. I now have a photocopy of this letter and my opinion is that it is a good simulation of KH's hand, but nevertheless a forgery. The literary style is unlike that of KH.

The Qualifications of Hodgson, Netherclift, and Sims

At this stage it is pertinent to inquire what were the qualifications and experience of Hodgson as an examiner of questioned documents. It is not clear from the records that he had either qualifications for or experience of the job. On the contrary, his methods suggest that he was untrained and illogical, with little sense of justice. Madame Blavatsky puts it very well when she refers to —

> Mr. Hodgson's elaborate but misdirected inquiries, his affected precision, which spends infinite patience over trifles and is blind to facts of importance, his contradictory reasoning and his manifest incapacity to deal with such problems as those he endeavored to solve. . . .
> — *H. P. Blavatsky: Collected Writings* 7:9

The reported opinions of Netherclift and Sims must be disregarded insofar as they relate to the Mahatma Letters. I repeat: we have no *written and signed* report from either of them, only Hodgson's version of what he says they had told him. The documents submitted to them cannot be identified. They changed their opinions under duress from Hodgson. Finally, and importantly, no suspect other than HPB was considered. No Court would accept such testimony.

---

*Michael Gomes, "The Coulomb Case 1884–1984," *The Theosophist*, December 1984, January 1985, February 1985, pp. 95-102, 138-47, 178-86.

## The KH Scripts

Let us now have a look at the main features of this series of scripts.

*General features*: The following general features are found throughout the whole series:

>The writing has a forward slant of about 30° to the vertical.
>
>The height of the body of the small letters (excluding ascenders and descenders) is remarkably uniform. Let us denote this height by H.
>
>The ascenders rise to a height of about 2H above the baseline, and the descenders extend to about 1H below the baseline.
>
>The space between lines is about 3½H.
>
>The height of the capitals is about 3H.
>
>The space between words is around 2H.
>
>The writing is flowing, unhurried, and carefully made.
>
>Pressure from word to word is even.
>
>Crossbars of the *t*'s are a prominent feature. They are long, sometimes excessively long, with a slight rise towards the right.
>
>Dots over the *i*'s are carefully placed close to the upward projection of the stem of the *i*.

*Stable characters persisting throughout the series*: There are a few highly characteristic letters which are found right from the start and persist throughout the whole KH series. They are:

> *h*  which reads like *li* without a dot, thus *li* .
>
> *p*  which usually looks like a hairpin with the right prong shortened and having a little downward curve added to the extremity, thus *p* .
>
> *n*  with its deeply troughed "garland" form which makes it indistinguishable from *u*, and
>
> *x*  which takes the Elizabethan form *x* .

*Characters variable in earliest scripts*: The rest of the letters are fairly stable with the exception of five: *f, g, k, t* and *y*. These exhibit a variety of forms in the early Letters, but they stabilize rapidly in the course of a few weeks.

I now recall Hodgson's FIRST CARDINAL PROPOSITION:

> That there are clear signs of development in the K.H. writing, various strong resemblances to Madame Blavatsky's ordinary handwriting having been gradually eliminated. — p.283

Writing of the earliest letter received by Mr. Sinnett (Barker's Letter 1, our Figure 12), Hodgson states:

> In this, which was received about October, 1880, the traces of Madame Blavatsky's handiwork were numerous and conspicuous, and from this onwards the gradual development of the K.H. conventional characteristics, and the gradual elimination of many of Madame Blavatsky's peculiarities, were clearly manifest. The K.H. writings which had been submitted to Mr. Netherclift [for examination], were written after Madame Blavatsky had had years of practice. — pp. 282-3

These statements are flatly contradicted by the direct evidence that has been preserved for us, including the Hodgson Report itself. We now look at some of the KH Letters in detail.

FIGURE 12  LETTER 1
Barker, p. 5  Slide No. K36015
RECEIVED at Simla on or about 15 October 1880

DAY 0

This is a page from the first Letter that Sinnett received at Simla on or about 15 October 1880 — identified as the one referred to in the Hodgson Report as K.H. No. 1. The writing is more untidy and a little harder to read than in the KH Letters which follow. There is a noticeable difference of "feel" compared with the later scripts. The letters are less rounded and regular; but the general features and stable characters are there from the start. As for the variable letters we find:

*f*   This is made only with the lower loop or with no loop at all.

*g*   This takes a multiplicity of forms. In Figure 12 we find

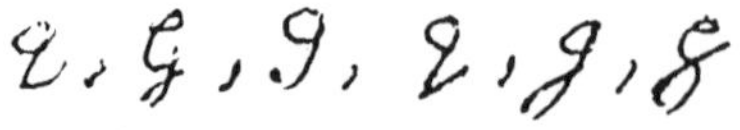

*[handwritten g forms]*. Some other forms occur in the

# PLATES
## Figures 11–22

Reproduced by permission of The British Library,
Additional MSS 45284, 45285, 45286 (Mahatma Papers)

that holy feeling that alone survives, and — not the slightest recollection of any other events or scenes? Love and
Hatred are the only immortal feelings, the only survivors
from the wreck of Ye-dhamma, or the phenomenal world. Ima-
gine yourself then, in Devachan with those you may
have loved with such immortal love; with the familiar shadowy scenes connected with them for a background
and — a perfect blank for everything else relating to
your interior, social, political, literary and social life.
And then, in the face of that spiritual, purely cogi-
tative existence, of that unalloyed felicity which, in
proportion with the intensity of the feeling that created
it, lasts from a few to several thousand years — call
it the "personal remembrance of A. P. Sinnett" — if you
can. Dreadfully monotonous! — you may think. — Not
in the least — I answer. Have you experienced mo-
notony during — say — that moment which you considered

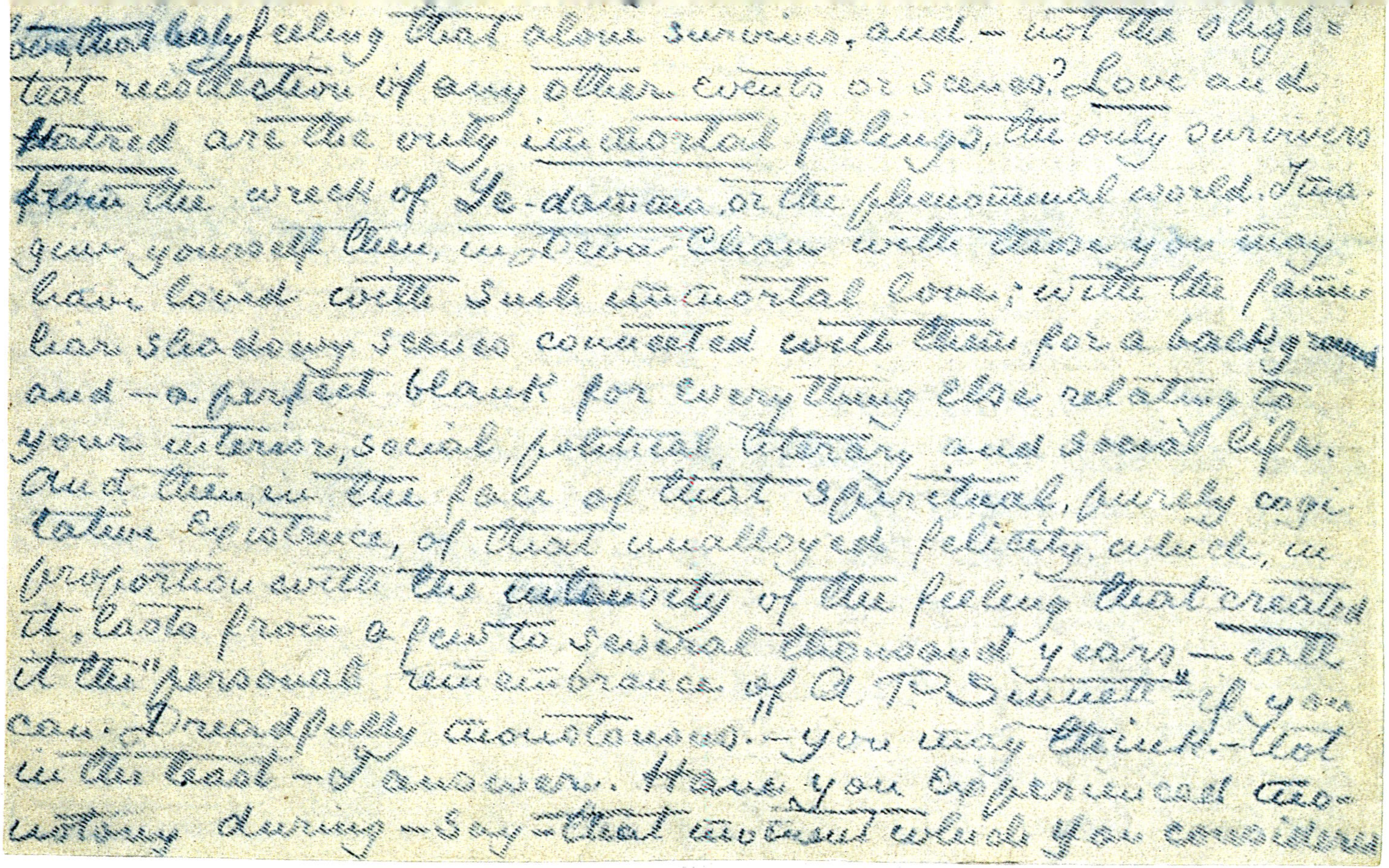

FIGURE 11
Letter 20c, received August 1882, KH script, approx. 8¼″ x 5½″ (scale 90%), see pages 31, 45, 68.

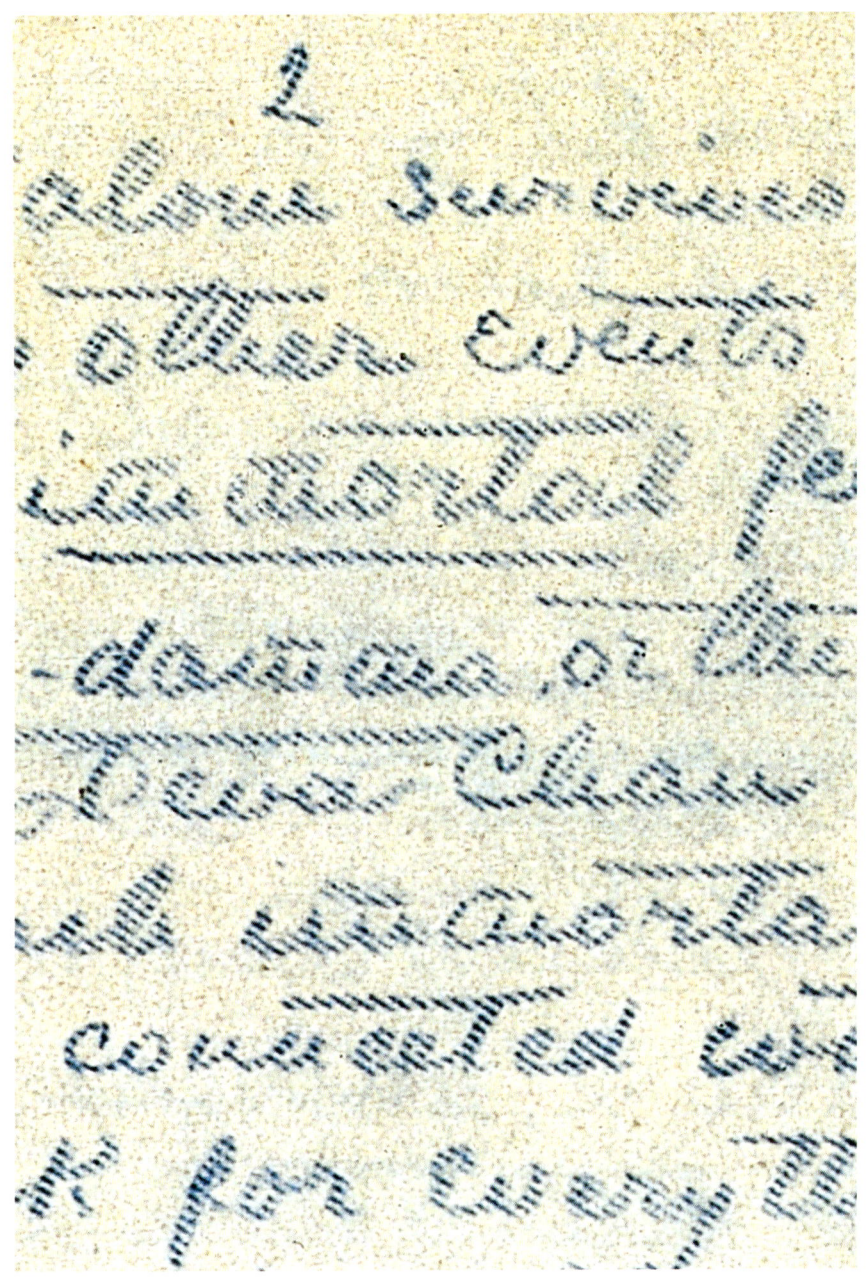

Figure 11 (enlarged detail)
Letter 20c, received August 1882, KH script, scale approx. 270%, see pages 31, 45, 68.

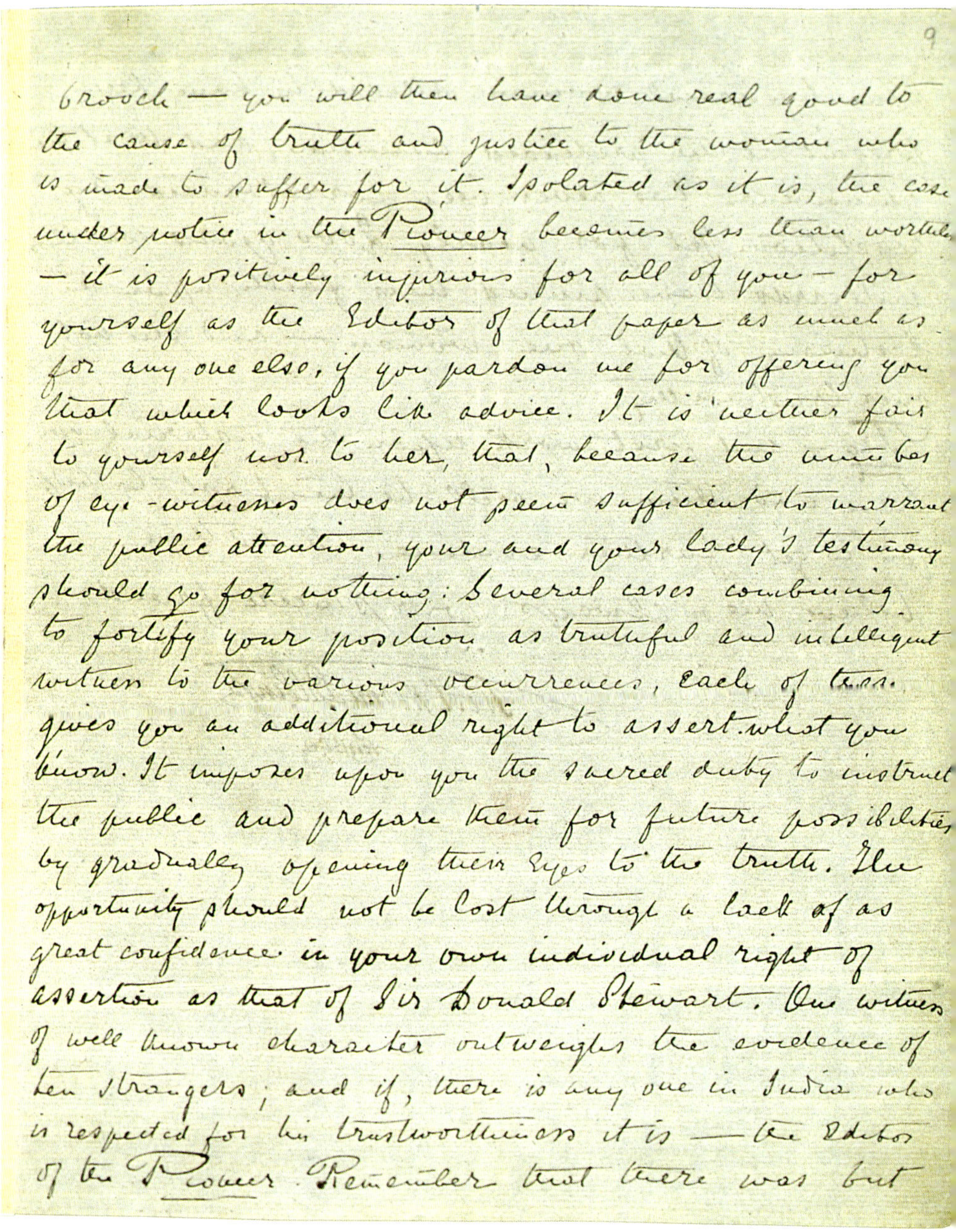

brooch — you will then have done real good to the cause of truth and justice to the woman who is made to suffer for it. Isolated as it is, the case under notice in the *Pioneer* becomes less than worthless — it is positively injurious for all of you — for yourself as the Editor of that paper as much as for any one else, if you pardon me for offering you that which looks like advice. It is neither fair to yourself nor to her, that, because the number of eye-witnesses does not seem sufficient to warrant the public attention, your and your lady's testimony should go for nothing: Several cases combining to fortify your position as truthful and intelligent witness to the various occurrences, each of them gives you an additional right to assert what you know. It imposes upon you the sacred duty to instruct the public and prepare them for future possibilities, by gradually opening their eyes to the truth. The opportunity should not be lost through a lack of as great confidence in your own individual right of assertion as that of Sir Donald Stewart. One witness of well known character outweighs the evidence of ten strangers; and if, there is any one in India who is respected for his trustworthiness it is — the Editor of the *Pioneer*. Remember that there was but

FIGURE 12

Letter 1, received c. October 15, 1880, KH script, 8¼″ x 10¼″ (scale 65%), see page 48.

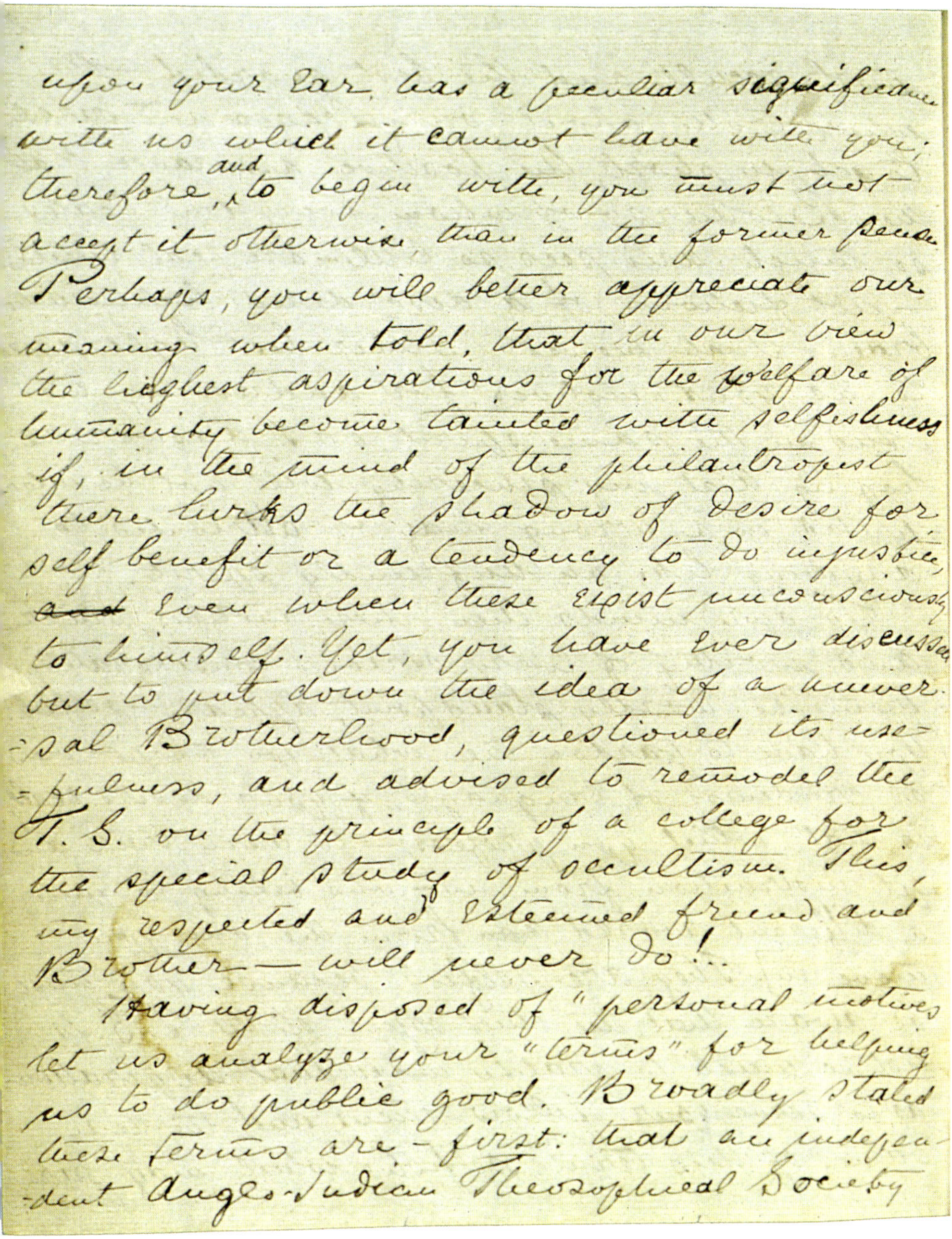

upon your ear, has a peculiar significance with us which it cannot have with you; therefore, and to begin with, you must not accept it otherwise, than in the former sense. Perhaps, you will better appreciate our meaning when told, that in our view the highest aspirations for the welfare of humanity become tainted with selfishness if, in the mind of the philanthropist there lurks the shadow of desire for self benefit or a tendency to do injustice, even when these exist unconsciously to himself. Yet, you have ever discussed but to put down the idea of a universal Brotherhood, questioned its usefulness, and advised to remodel the T. S. on the principle of a college for the special study of occultism. This, my respected and esteemed friend and Brother — will never do!

Having disposed of "personal motives" let us analyze your "terms" for helping us to do public good. Broadly stated these terms are, — first: that an independent Anglo-Indian Theosophical Society

FIGURE 13

Letter 2, received October 19, 1880, KH script, 8¼" x 10¼" (scale 65%), see page 49.

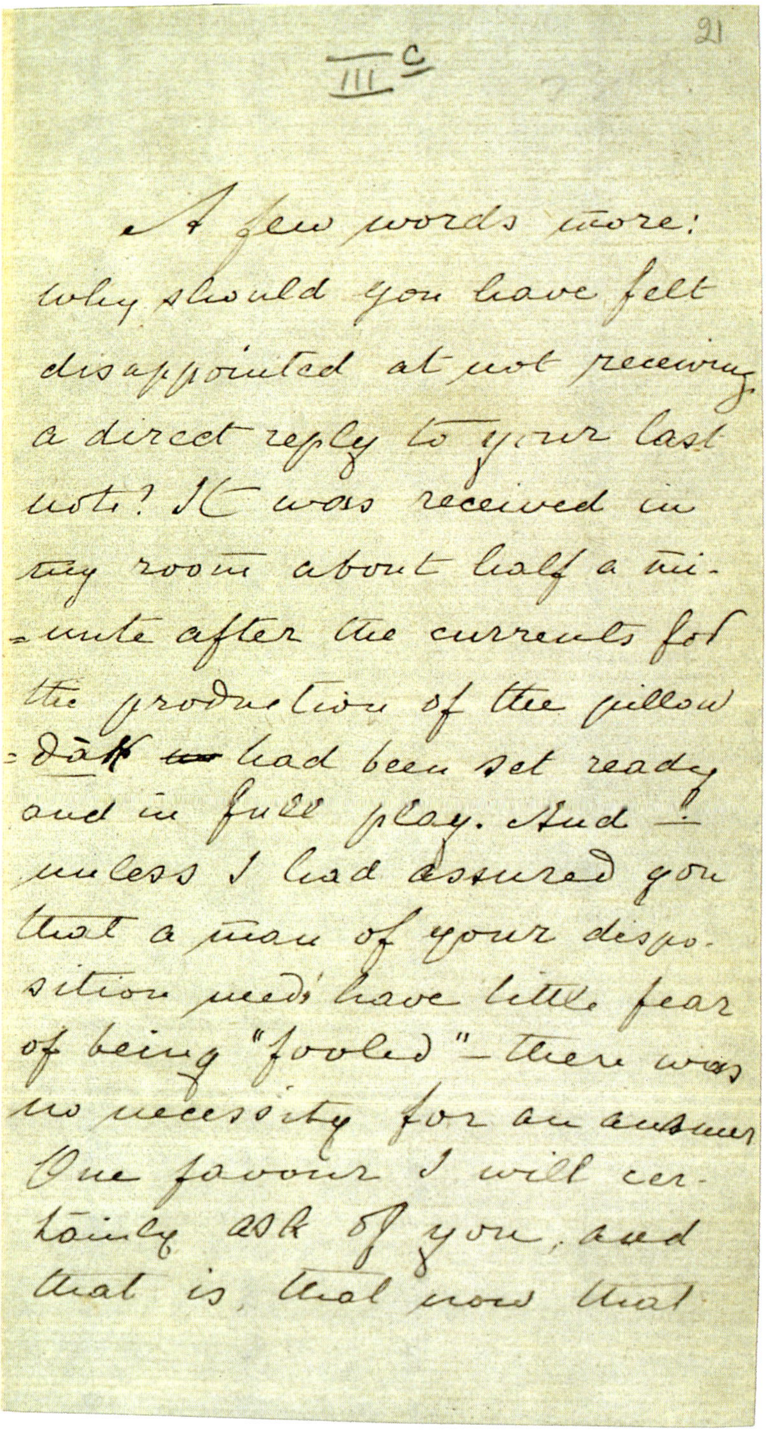

III.c

A few words more: why should you have felt disappointed at not receiving a direct reply to your last note? It was received in my room about half a minute after the currents for the production of the pillow dâk had been set ready and in full play. And — unless I had assured you that a man of your disposition need have little fear of being "fooled" — there was no necessity for an answer. One favour I will certainly ask of you, and that is, that now that

FIGURE 14
Letter 3c, received c. October 20, 1880, KH script, 4⅛″ x 7½″
(scale 100%), see page 49.

shall not be allowed to disconnect itself with the Parent Body, tho' you are at liberty to manage your affairs in your own way without fearing the slightest interference from its President so long as you do not violate the general Rules. And upon this point I refer you to Rule IX. This is the first practical suggestion coming from a Cis and Trans-Himalayan "Cave=dweller" whom you have honoured with your confidence.

And now about yourself personally. Far be it from me to discourage one so willing as yourself by setting up impossible barriers to your progress. We never whine over the inevitable but try to make the best of the worst. And tho' we neither push nor draw into the mysterious domain of occult nature those who are unwilling; never ~~refuse~~ shrink from expressing our opinions freely and fearlessly, yet we are ever as ready to assist those who come to us; even to agnostics who assume the negative position of "knowing nothing but phenomena and refuse to believe in anything else." It is true that the married man cannot be an adept, yet without striving to become a "Raj Yogi" he can acquire certain powers

FIGURE 15

Letter 4, dated October 29, 1880, KH script, 8¼" x 10¼" (scale 65%), see page 50.

They teach man's true position in the universe, in relation to his previous and future births; his origin and ultimate destiny; the relation of the mortal to the immortal, of the temporary to the Eternal, of the finite to the Infinite; ideas larger, grander, more comprehensive, recognizing the universal reign of immutable law, including and unchangeable in regard to which there is but only an Eternal Now, which to uninitiated mortals time is past or future, as related to their finite existence on this material speck of dirt. This is which will you have: the highest philosophy or simple Exhibitions of occult powers. Of course this is by far not the last word between us and — you will have time to think it over. The Chiefs want a "Bro̅= therhood of Humanity," a real Universal Fraternity started; an institution which would make itself known throughout the world and arrest the attention of the highest minds. I will send you my Essay. Will you be my co-worker and patiently wait for

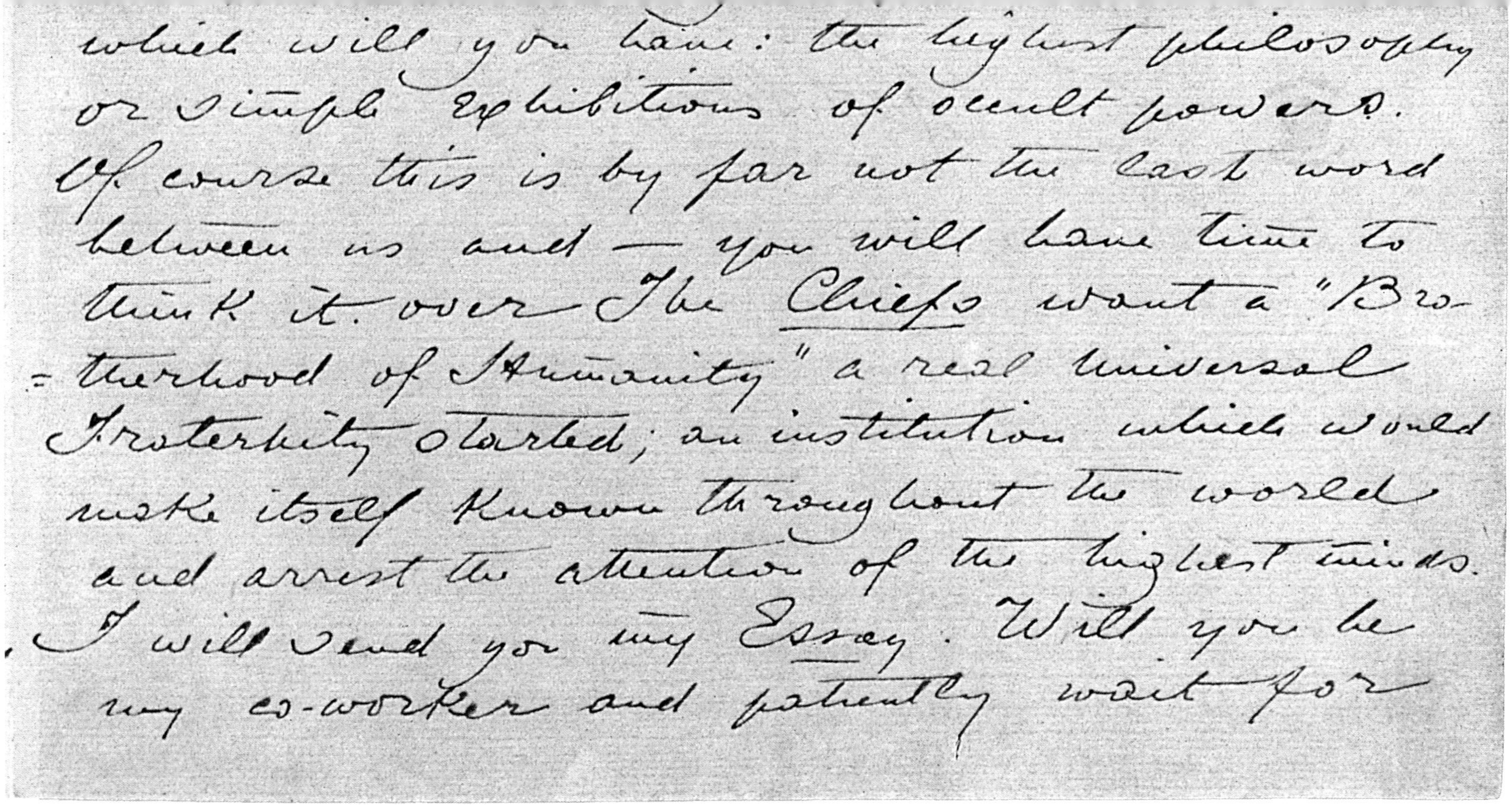

FIGURE 16

Letter 6, received c. December 10, 1880, KH script, 8½" x 10½" (scale 100%), see page 51.

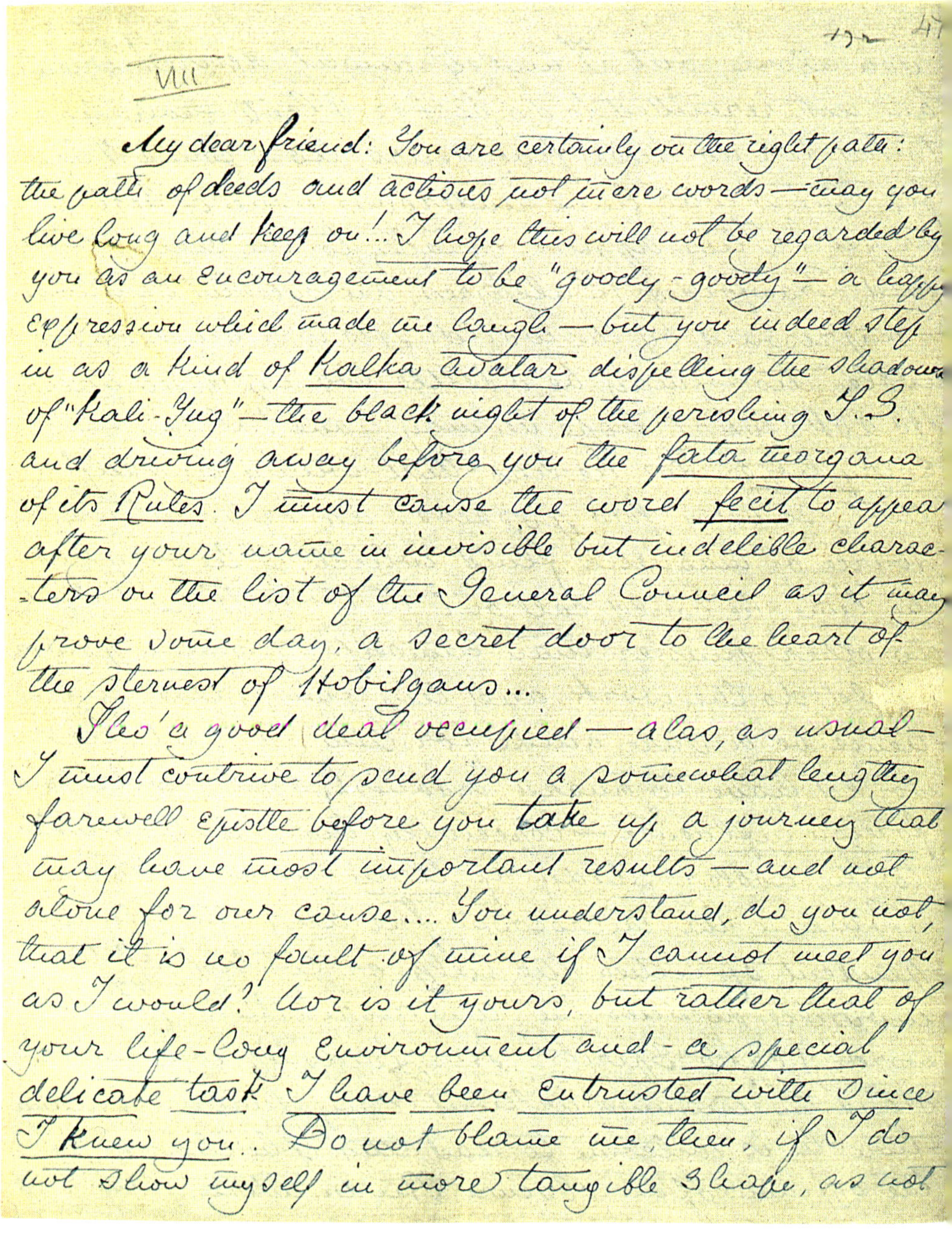

VIII

My dear friend: You are certainly on the right path: the path of deeds and actions not mere words — may you live long and keep on!... I hope this will not be regarded by you as an encouragement to be "goody-goody" — a happy expression which made me laugh — but you indeed step in as a kind of Kalka avatar dispelling the shadows of "Kali-Yug" — the black night of the perishing T.S. and driving away before you the fata morgana of its Rules. I must cause the word fecit to appear after your name in invisible but indelible characters on the list of the General Council as it may prove some day, a secret door to the heart of the sternest of Hobilgans...

I's a good deal occupied — alas, as usual — I must contrive to send you a somewhat lengthy farewell epistle before you take up a journey that may have most important results — and not alone for our cause.... You understand, do you not, that it is no fault of mine if I cannot meet you as I would? Nor is it yours, but rather that of your life-long environment and - a special delicate task I have been entrusted with since I knew you. Do not blame me, then, if I do not show myself in more tangible shape, as not

FIGURE 17

Letter 8, received c. February 20, 1881, KH script, 8½″ x 10½″ (scale 63%), see page 51.

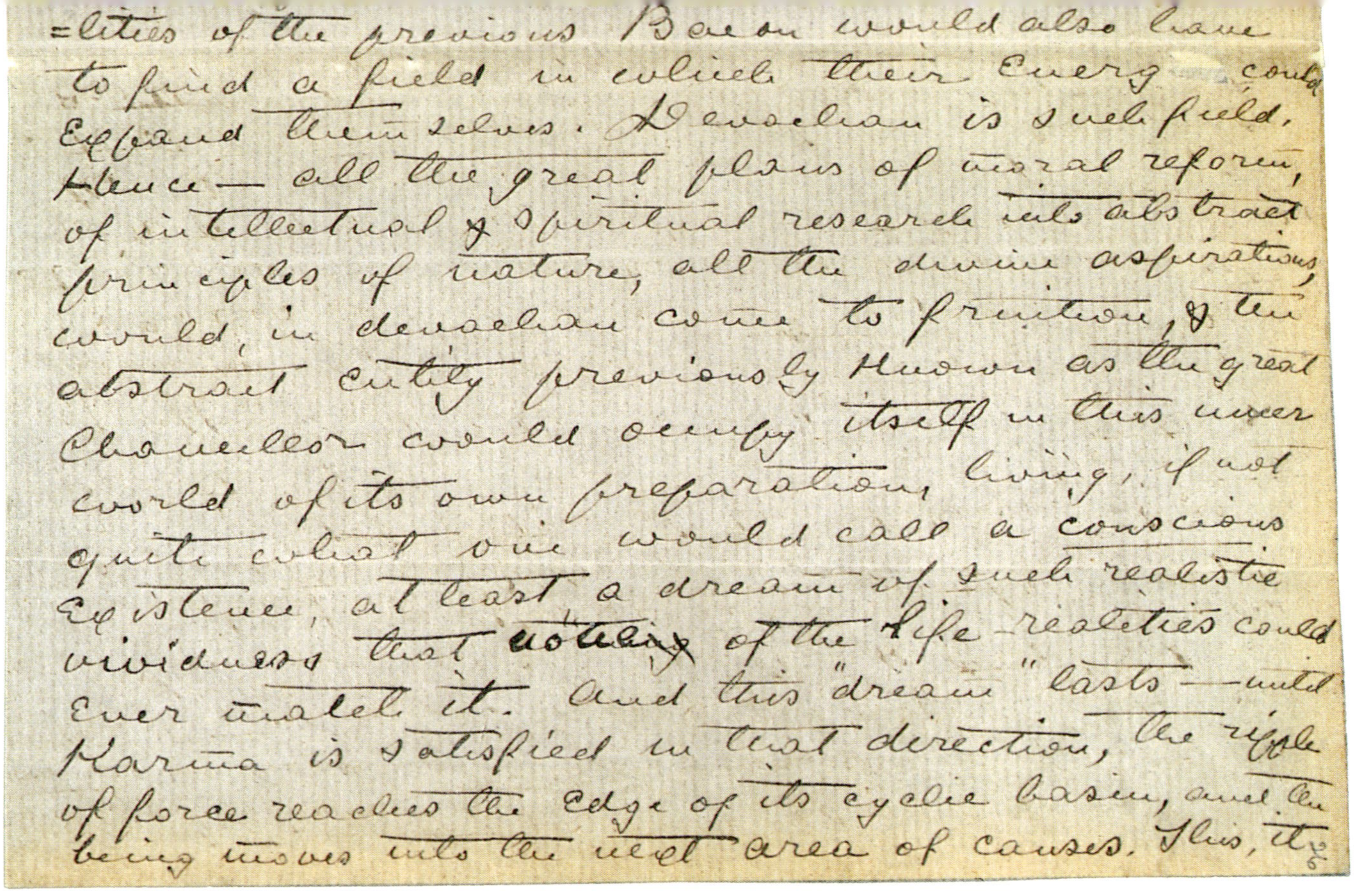
=lities of the previous Bacon would also have
to find a field in which their energy could
expand themselves. Devachan is such field.
Hence — all the great plans of moral reform,
of intellectual & spiritual research into abstract
principles of nature, all the divine aspirations,
would, in devachan come to fruition, & the
abstract entity previously known as the great
Chancellor would occupy itself in this inner
world of its own preparation, living, if not
quite what one would call a conscious
existence, at least a dream of such realistic
vividness that nothing of the life-realities could
ever match it. And this "dream" lasts — until
Karma is satisfied in that direction, the ripple
of force reaches the edge of its cyclic basin, and the
being moves into the next area of causes. This, it

FIGURE 18

Letter 25, received February 2, 1883, KH script, approx 8¼″ wide (scale 85%), see page 51.

And now for a few parting words by explanation. As
prev— which produced such disastrous results of a most
adverse que prologue was written on the 27th. On the night of the
25th my beloved brother told me, that having heard Mrs. Luan
say in St. P.B's room that he had pernd himself heard O stat
to him that he O. had pernately seen us, and also had
heard AOO that there clerk to tell him it, he had confidence
enough in the man to believe in what he said — be it R.L.
thought of making me to go of the O, to do so, believing
it might please Mr. Luan to learn from us of the Desaets
of L. mishaas — came to me. And there is why Mr. Luan
received that letter from O., at a time when his Doubt
were already settled. When he drew them as if delivered
any one page to P. J. Retalshed this cerrcut as to order

That is the truth. The secret pleasures of my own I think you should know what I thought of the letter. A few lines after my beloved Brother meant less of this world when the letter reached you. My feelings are somewhat changed & I altered, as said before the name of good Perl. As it's still had made me change. I need my past Scriptures which related solely to that, but was generated up applied wholly by him that we be himself.

Let no day of — if close the longest letter I have ever written in my life, but as I do it, for half — I am satisfied. Though you have may not think it, the mark of the abbot is kept at — and at Simla, & I try to keep up to it, however poor I may be to a writer to correspondents.

J.M.S.

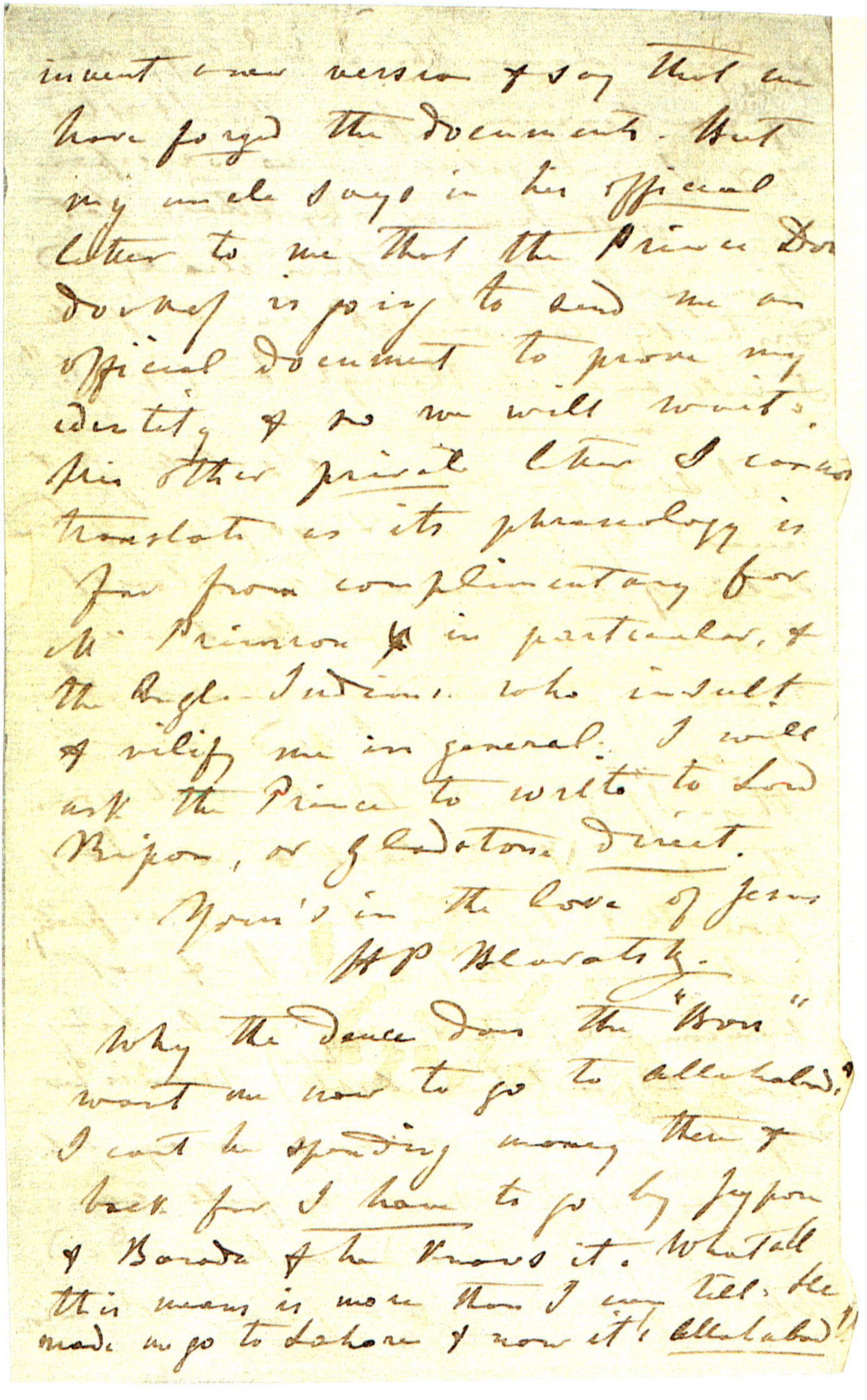

invent a new version & say that we have forged the documents. That my uncle says in his official letter to me that the Prince Dondukoff is going to send me an official document to prove my identity, & so we will wait. His other private letter I could not translate as its phraseology is far from complimentary for Mr Primrose & in particular, & the Anglo-Indians who insult & vilify me in general. I will ask the Prince to write to Lord Ripon, or Gladstone direct.

Yours in the love of Jesus
HP Blavatsky.

Why the deuce does the "Boss" want me now to go to Allahabad? I cant be spending money there & back for I have to go by Jypore & Baroda & he knows it. What all this means is more than I can tell. He made us go to Lahore & now it's Allahabad!!

FIGURE 20

Letter 134, dated Dehra Dun Friday 4th, HPB's script, 5¼″ x 8¼″ (scale 89%), see page 55.

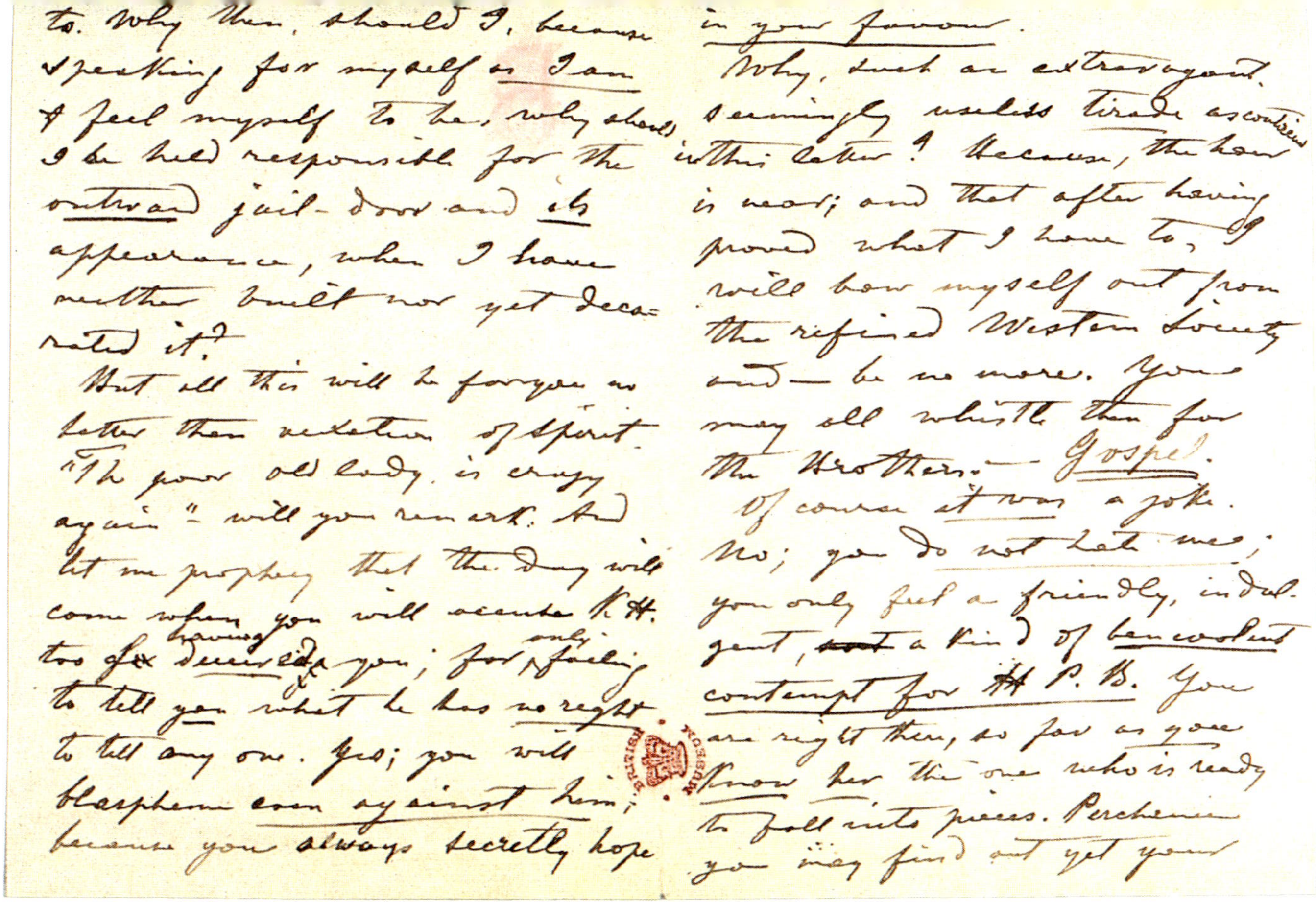

FIGURE 21

Letter 136, dated March 17th, HPB's script, approximate scale 80%, see page 55.

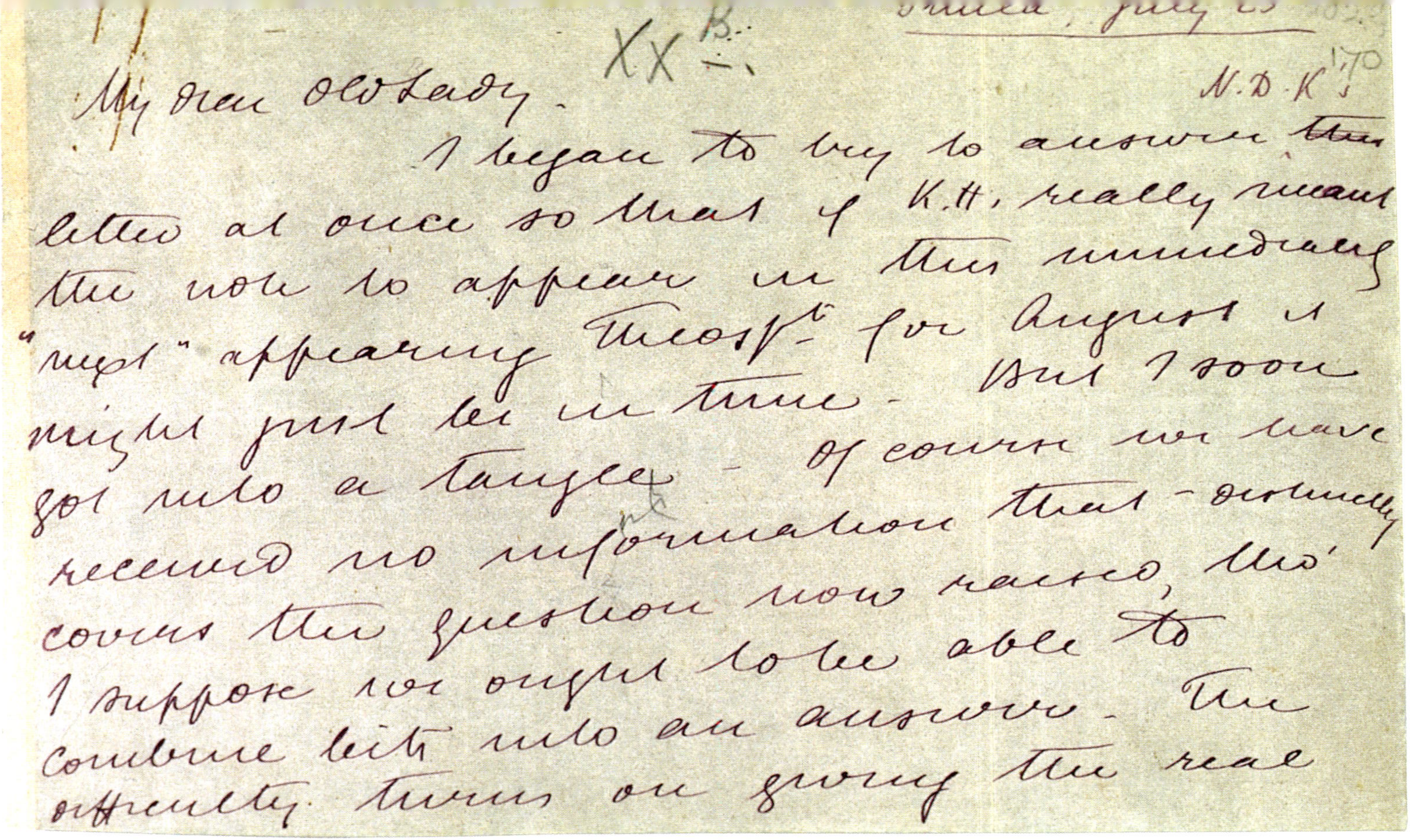
XX B.
N.D.K.
170
My dear Old Lady.
I began to try to answer this
letter at once so that if K.H. really meant
the note to appear in this immediately
"next" appearing Theosoph[t] for August it
might just be in time. But I soon
got into a tangle — Of course we have
received no information that directly
covers the question now raised, tho'
I suppose we ought to be able to
combine bits into an answer. The
difficulty turns on giving the real

FIGURE 22

Letter 20b, received August 1882, Sinnett's script, 8¼" x 5¼" (scale 97%), see page 57.

pages of this Letter which are not illustrated. We shall see later that none of these forms is particularly Blavatskian with the exception of *g* and *g*. Far from being exclusively Blavatskian, the first of these is common enough, and the second is of ancient lineage, being common in the Elizabethan Secretary Script.

*y*  This occurs in the forms *y , y y . y*. The second of these is the Blavatskian form, but there is nothing unusual about it.

It should be mentioned at this point that cases where a writer makes the same letter in two or more distinctive forms, apparently haphazardly, are frequent. Many writers make the letter *e* in the forms *e* and *ε*, and *d* in the forms *d* and *∂*; and the alternatives can be found on the same page or even within the same word.

---

FIGURE 13  LETTER 2
Barker, p. 8  Slide No. K36023
RECEIVED at Simla 19 October 1880

### DAY 4

This arrived only four days later than Letter 1, and it is already a more elegant script. We find:

*f*  appears either with the lower loop only or with both loops.

*g*  The form *g* is preferred throughout the extract.

*y*  *y* and *y* are still preferred, but *y* and *y* make their appearance.

---

FIGURE 14  LETTER 3c
Barker, p. 11  Slide No. K36034
RECEIVED about 20 October 1880

### DAY 5

*f* appears either with the lower loop only or with both loops.

*g* Forms *g* and *g* make their appearance.

*y* The form *y* is preferred, but we also have *y*, *y* and *y*.

---

FIGURE 15                     LETTER 4
Barker, pp. 16–17             Slide No. K36050
DATED 29 October 1880

DAY 14

*f* appears with the *upper* loop only.

*g* takes the forms *g*, *g*, *g*, *g*, *g*.

*y* *y* and *y* are preferred, but *y* now appears for the first time.

Thus, *within a fortnight*, we are very near the fully "developed" KH script.

---

FIGURE 2, Part 1
DATED 1 November 1880

This is part of Hodgson's K.H. (i) from a letter to Mr. A. O. Hume. It is not found in Barker, nor in the British Library's collection. The illustration is only a "facsimile" of the original, but it shows clearly that:

*f* is found with the upper loop only.

*g* takes the forms *g* and *g*.

*y* prefers the forms *y* and *y*, but *y* and *y* appear.

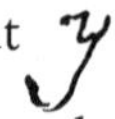

This is almost the final form of the script, dated *only a fortnight* after the arrival of Letter 1. This is taken from the Hodgson Report itself. So much for HPB's "years of practice."

Did Gurney, Myers & Co., and the generations who have followed them, *never* look critically at Hodgson's Report?

---

FIGURE 16   LETTER 6
Barker, p. 24   Slide No. K36070
RECEIVED about 10 December 1880
DAY 56

*f* appears with upper loop only.

*g* ⌣𝒢 is preferred, but 𝒢 and 𝑔 are also found.

*y* Forms 𝑦, 𝒴 and 𝓏 are found.

---

FIGURE 17   LETTER 8
Barker, p. 26   Slide No. K36078
RECEIVED about 20 February 1881
DAY 107

*f* appears with upper loop only or with both loops.

*g* Form ⌣𝒢 is used almost exclusively.

*y* Forms 𝒴, 𝒴, and 𝑦 are found.

This is an excellent example of the KH script with long crossbars to the *t*'s.

---

I conclude this section with one example of a later date.

FIGURE 18   LETTER 25
Barker, pp. 191-2 (2nd ed.), 189 (3rd ed.)
RECEIVED 2 February 1883   Slide No. K36496
DAY 840

The crossbars to the *t*'s are more pronounced here than in Letter 8, otherwise the script does not differ from it except in points of detail.

The transition from the instability in form of the earliest KH script to a stable script is yet another puzzling feature of these writings and the reason for it is not clear; but it certainly was not "gradual." It was almost completed within a fortnight. I do not find "numerous and conspicuous traces of Madame Blavatsky's handiwork" anywhere. Nor is it "manifest" that "Madame Blavatsky's peculiarities" were eliminated during a process of gradual development of the script. To be sure, a number of forms of *g* and *y* disappeared after the first few weeks of receiving the scripts, but these were not typically Blavatskian forms.

After Letter 7, the variations in the KH script are no more than one might expect of the same writer using different pens or pencils, and in different moods or states of health. The most conspicuous variations in later Letters are in the lengths of the crossbars to the *t*'s, which can become grotesquely long and spoil an otherwise graceful and legible script.

We come to Hodgson's SECOND CARDINAL PROPOSITION:

> That special forms of letters proper to Madame Blavatsky's ordinary writing, and not proper to the K.H. writing, occasionally appear in the latter.

This proposition does not amount to much. Hodgson refers vaguely to examples he has found in the documents in his possession, but I have found it impossible to track them down, and no examples are given.

There are many erasures and corrections in the Letters, but these are the work of a writer who, having second thoughts about a word or phrase, did not want to rewrite the whole sheet and did not have a word processor. You will find plenty of what Hodgson calls "additions, reformations, cloakings and erasures" in my own handwriting.

Hodgson states on page 287 of his report:

> The letter *e* in Madame Blavatsky's ordinary writing is uniformly made upon the common type which we are all taught in copybooks, but when it begins a word in the K.H. writing, it is formed on the same type as Madame Blavatsky's capital E in her ordinary writing. Yet in the early K.H. documents there are many instances where the initial small *e* was at first well formed in the ordinary way, and then transformed into the other type by the addition of a second curve at the top; there are instances also where the transformation was never made, and the initial *e* of the ordinary type still remains.

I have noticed a few examples of this type of alteration in the slides, but I have to say that the use of both types of *e* is widespread. *E* is the commonest letter in the English language; and *e* permits of fewer variations than do most other letters of the alphabet. There is nothing in these particular *e*'s that is *specially characteristic* of HPB. What possible justification had Hodgson for attributing them to Madame Blavatsky to the exclusion of all others? They could have been made by almost anyone, including KH himself.

Hodgson makes much of one or two rogue *x*'s which he has found in the documents in his hands. I cannot identify these documents in the slides, but a rogue *x* is found in the word "Quixottes" seen in K.H. (v) of Plate 3 of his report. This form is suggestive of HPB's *x*, but I cannot attach much weight to an isolated example. KH could easily have made a false start to the Elizabethan type of *x* that he normally uses and decided that it would be both easier and neater to cross the *x* in the Blavatskian manner in order to complete the letter.

Hodgson points out some similarities in the capital letters used by KH and HPB; but the similarities are not very close and the forms used are common enough. I do not think that they have any significance.

Hodgson's THIRD CARDINAL PROPOSITION is

> That there are certain very marked peculiarities of Madame Blavatsky's ordinary writing which occur throughout the K.H. writing. — p. 283

I hold this proposition to be demonstrably false; and as I have dealt with it largely in Part 1, there is no need to repeat what I have written. During my examination of the 1,323 color slides, I paid special attention to those which showed specimens of HPB's writing. I could not find *any single feature* of her handwriting which, if present in a manuscript, would prove her authorship beyond reasonable doubt. What Hodgson calls the "left-gap stroke" is found in other writers and is far less important than Hodgson thought it to be.

## The M Scripts

It is convenient at this point to describe the M series of Letters which Hodgson ignores. There are twenty-six of these in the British Library collection — fewer than the KH Letters, but quite enough to be important. The M Letters differ markedly both in handwriting and in literary style from the Letters of KH and HPB. KH writes an individual script which is, apart from some of the earliest Letters, graceful, legible, and easy to recognize. His style is aristocratic, courteous, rather formal and reserved, discursive and at times plain long-winded; but he is not without the occasional touch of humor. M's writing is quite different.

He usually prefers red ink. He dislikes writing, and says so. He is direct and terse, says what he has to say, and signs off. M is more down to earth than is KH; and the smile when he is writing is never far away. The scripts of both KH and M are far removed from the explosive bursts of HPB which suggest a Meteorological Office warning of the approach of Hurricane Helena.

As few can have seen M's Letters, I reproduce a typical sample in Figure 19. This will suffice as M's writing does not vary nearly as much as does KH's writing in his earliest Letters.

> FIGURE 19                          LETTER 29
> Barker, pp. 227-8 (2nd ed.), 225 (3rd ed.)
> Undated                            Slide No. K36592

This is the last page of a long letter.

MAIN FEATURES OF M'S WRITING

*General.*

> The most striking characteristic of M's script is the "regular irregularity" of the small letters. Some, like r, are consistently larger than the average, while others, notably e, are smaller than the average. It is therefore hard to estimate the mean height (H) of the body of the small letters. They do not fit neatly between two parallel lines as do the characters of KH. This feature gives the writing strong individuality.
>
> The slant of the writing is consistent and about 40° forward from the vertical, significantly greater than in the KH scripts.
>
> Despite the variability of the small letters, they generally keep to the baseline.
>
> The writing is carefully made and flowing, but not all the letters within a word are connected.
>
> The height of the capitals is about 2½H.
>
> The lines are more closely spaced than in KH's writing — about 3H.
>
> The pen pressure from word to word is even.

*Some Characteristic Letters.* Some letter formations of particular interest are:

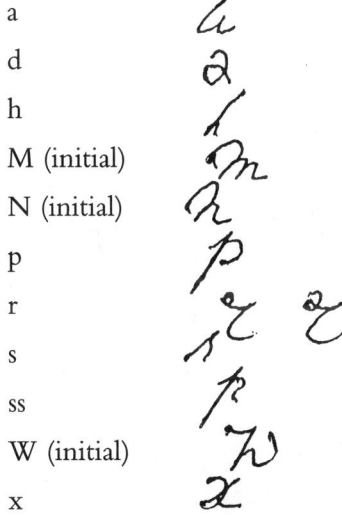

a
d
h
M (initial)
N (initial)
p
r
s
ss
W (initial)
x

In addition, *g* and *y* are often disproportionately small.

## H. P. Blavatsky's Script

I now take for examination extracts from two Letters from HPB preserved in the British Library collection. The particulars are:

FIGURE 20      LETTER 134
Barker, pp. 463-4 (2nd ed.), 456-7 (3rd ed.)
DATED: Dehra Dun Friday 4th      Slide No. K37262

FIGURE 21      LETTER 136
Barker, pp. 466 (2nd ed.), 458-9 (3rd ed.)
DATED: March 17th      Slide No. K37268

MAIN FEATURES OF HPB'S WRITING
*General.*

There is a powerful drive about this writing. It is rapid, but mostly legible though one has to depend upon context more than in the KH and M scripts. There are wide variations in the pressure applied to the pen, and strong downward pressure is particularly noticeable in letters like *d* and *p*. This can be discerned even in the slides. The effect of pressure is completely lost in the facsimiles of Hodgson's Plate 2, which thereby give a misleading impression of the writing as a whole.

The slant of the writing is about 45° to the right of the vertical. It reaches 50° on occasion.

The body of the small letters is small (sometimes vanishingly small) compared with their spacing.

By comparison with the body height, the ascenders and descenders of the small letters are long. Descenders may reach 6H, ascenders 4H.

The height of the capitals is estimated at about 3H and the distance between lines at 3H.

*Some Characteristic Letters.* Noteworthy are:

b
d
g
h
m
n
p
x

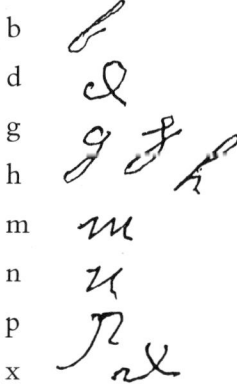

See also the comparison table of letter formations set out on page 59.

*Comparison of Scripts by KH, M, and HPB.* I find no evidence of common authorship of the KH, M, and HPB scripts. Comparison of their general features, which Hodgson ignored, as well as the detailed construction of individual letters, shows that these are three different writings. I attribute them to different writers.

## A. P. Sinnett's Script

In his efforts to implicate HPB it seems never to have occurred to Hodgson that one should have a look at the writing of other possible suspects before concluding. One possible suspect is A. P. Sinnett himself. His two books, *The Occult World* and *Esoteric Buddhism*, proved to be best sellers, and it could be argued that he forged the Mahatma Letters in order to provide spurious authority to his work. This is at any rate a more plausible motive than Hodgson's suggestion that HPB forged the Letters in order to foment insurrection in British India.

Sinnett's script is shown in Figure 22, and the particulars are:

FIGURE 22                              LETTER 20b
Barker, pp. 125 (2nd ed.), 121-2 (3rd ed.)
DATED: Simla July 25th          Slide No. K36266
RECEIVED August 1882

If we compare Sinnett's writing in Figure 22 with KH's writing in Figure 17 we see that there are numerous similarities. Sinnett's writing is more angular than KH's and it is more stretched in the horizontal direction. However, it is much nearer in style to KH's than is HPB's.

MAIN FEATURES OF A. P. SINNETT'S SCRIPT

*General*

The slant is about 30° from the vertical, forward.

The height of the body of the small letters (H) is fairly uniform.

The ascenders rise to about 1¾H above the baseline and the descenders dip to about 2H below the baseline. They are less prominent than they are in the KH script.

The height of the capitals is about 2H.

The space between lines is about 3H and the space between words is about the same.

These rough measurements and the general "feel" of the writing are enough to show that it could have been much easier for Sinnett to adapt his writing to the KH style than it would have been for HPB to do so.

58 / *H. P. Blavatsky and the SPR*

*Comparison of Individual Letters with KH's.* Compare the following:

| Letter | KH's writing (Fig. 17) | | APS's writing (Fig. 22) | |
|--------|-----------|------------|-----------|------------|
| c | (Line 5) | received | (Line 3) | once |
| | (Line 7) | currents | (Line 9) | covers |
| d | (Line 1) | dear | (Line 8) | production |
| g | (Line 3) | receiving | (Line 2) | began |
| th | (Line 14) | there | (Line 4) | this |
| n | (Line 3) | not | (Line 3) | once |
| | | | (Line 7) | tangle |
| p | (Line 4) | reply | (Line 4) | appearing |
| | (Line 8) | production | | |
| x | See Fig. 15, line 18, | | (Line 5) | next |
| | | expressing | | |

Accepting these similarities, rejecting all differences and investing the letter *p* with the importance of Hodgson's "left-gap stroke," I could make a case for Sinnett's authorship of the Mahatma Letters. This illustrates the importance of looking at the handwriting of as many suspects as possible before pronouncing judgment. Hodgson never considered any suspect other than HPB.

However, Sinnett may rest in peace. His writing is not the same as KH's, despite the similarities.

# Faults in Spelling, Hyphenation, and Structure

On pages 306 and 307 of his report, Hodgson seeks to reinforce his case by citing mistakes of spelling, grammar, style, and hyphenation found in the pages of both KH and HPB. I find this section wholly unconvincing. The most that these mistakes show is that the two writers were not quite familiar with the English language. We knew this already. Since the mistakes are common and widespread, what they do not show is identity of KH and HPB.

There can be but few aspects of the writer's craft which authors understand less than that of hyphenation at the end of lines. You will find elaborate rules for hyphenation in the preamble to *Webster's New*

## Comparison Table of Letter Formations
### found in the KH, M, HPB, and APS Scripts

| | KH | M | HPB | APS |
|---|---|---|---|---|
| a | | | | |
| b | | | | |
| c | | | | |
| d | | | | |
| e | | | | |
| f | | | | |
| g | | | | |
| h | | | | |
| i | | | | |
| j | | | | |
| k | | | | |
| l | | | | |
| m | | | | |
| n | | | | |
| o | | | | |
| p | | | | |
| q | | | | |
| r | | | | |
| s | | | | |
| t | | | | |
| u | | | | |
| v | | | | |
| w | | | | |
| x | | | | |
| y | | | | |
| z | | | | |

One should always remember that the writing as a whole, as well as the formation of individual letters, is important when judging a piece of handwriting.

## 60 / *H. P. Blavatsky and the SPR*

*International Dictionary* of 1928, but I can never remember what they are. This does not worry me because if my work is intended for publication, hyphenation, if needed, will be made by the compositor or a computer, no matter what I write. To advance the faults of hyphenation shown on page 306 of the Hodgson Report as evidence of the identity of KH and HPB is ridiculous.

HPB did not start to write in English until quite late in life, and she did so because she thought that her work would be more widely read in this language. She needed help at first. It is not surprising that her earlier work in English shows a French influence.

I do not know what KH's linguistic background was, but it also shows a French influence. As French was, and still is, a world language, this does not prove much.

Hodgson never misses an opportunity of sneering at HPB's English. One would think from his remarks that both KH and HPB wrote in a sort of Pidgin English. This is not so. KH's style, though a little formal, is generally good, and his occasional lapses are no more than most of us make from time to time in the first draft of a document. He himself made many corrections to his Letters on points of wording and style.

Having read the original, unedited, holograph KH Letters, I find this section of the Hodgson Report quite deplorable. It illustrates argument by innuendo.

# Replies to Criticism

During the preparation of this work for publication I have received comments and criticisms, the which to answer I find convenient to put into the form of a dialogue.

CRITIC: If you look at Olcott's *Old Diary Leaves* you will find abundant evidence that HPB acted in the manner of a medium, put into trance states, etc., and that above all she was accustomed to writing long, indeed very long, passages in writings very different from her normal writing. This being so, I do not see how you can possibly establish the independence of the KH, M, and HPB writings just on the basis of analyzing a few specimens of HPB's "ordinary" writing.

VH: First, let me remind you that Hodgson's whole thesis was that HPB was *an ingenious but common fraudster and impostor having no supernormal powers whatsoever.* The KH Letters, he maintains, were written in a disguised form of her ordinary writing, a disguise acquired deliberately by practice over several years. To write such letters with intent to deceive can be, and usually is, a criminal offense. Writing received automatically, in trance, sleep, etc., unknown to the conscious personality until he or she reads it, does not involve deception and is not a culpable offense though it might be considered a case for psychiatric examination. There is a world of difference here that you fail to distinguish.

Second, the "few" specimens of HPB's "ordinary" writing to which you refer are nine letters preserved in the British Library. All are originals, not copies or facsimiles. All are complete and signed or initialed by HPB. All are written reasonably near in time to the period of the Mahatma Letters. All are consistent, both in handwriting and in literary style. Letter 138 tops 4,000 words and is HPB's farewell letter, written *de profundis*, to Mr. and Mrs. Sinnett. I have every reason to believe that all this is a good specimen of her ordinary, normal writing of the time, produced by her conscious volition, writing that she used for

62 / *H. P. Blavatsky and the SPR*

correspondence with friends, setting out her laundry list and giving instructions to the Coulombs.

The KH, M, and HPB scripts are quite different and, if they cropped up in any ordinary legal case, I would certainly attribute them to different persons. Whether trance personalities are independent of the conscious personalities is another matter.

Third, if we accept Olcott's testimony as evidence that HPB could write in altered states of consciousness, do we accept his further testimony in *Old Diary Leaves* (3rd revised edition, 2:365-7) that, in response to a request made on the spur of the moment, she received a letter precipitated on a blank sheet of paper held between her hands, from a person she had not met, in writing to her unknown? Do we accept this, and, if not, why not? I do not see how you can select or reject evidence to suit your argument: we are not politicians. Olcott's testimony is that HPB possessed psychic powers in abundance. You cannot accept both Olcott and Hodgson.

Please to remember that whenever I have been able to check Hodgson's statements against the direct testimony of the original documents preserved for us in the British Library, I have found Hodgson's statements to be false; and I have given my reasons why. They would still be false were the Mahatma Letters written by Helena Petrovna Blavatsky or Assur-bani-pal. They would be false whether the letters were written in normal consciousness, in trance, sleep, automatically, or in any other altered state of consciousness. These falsities are not trivial: they give the lie to the three cardinal statements on which Hodgson's thesis concerning the Mahatma Letters depends.

*CRITIC*: There is a need for these sorts of comparisons to be carried out by experts who can be assumed to have no preconceptions, who do not know what the "right" answer is. I don't believe that anyone, in any field of science, can be totally immune to the influence of prior expectations and hopes and I think that double blind methodologies should be used wherever possible.

*VH*: If we were asked to judge, by hearing it, whether the "Sophie Menter" piano concerto was written, not by Sophie Menter, but composed by Liszt and orchestrated by Tchaikowsky, I would agree with you. However, here we are classifying the geometrical outlines of cer-

*Replies to Criticism* / 63

tain individual letters by criteria capable of definition in terms of differential geometry.

If I gave you and others a selection of five hundred assorted triangles and asked you to deal them out into equilateral, isosceles, right-angled, and scalene, I would expect a large measure of agreement among you. Even Aunt Matilda would get the same result if she were shown what to look for.

Here I am asking you to classify the geometrical forms of certain letters according to definable characteristics. In the letter *g* we can notice whether it has a "tail" or ends in a straight down stroke; if it has a "tail," is it curved to the left or to the right; does it form an open or closed loop; is the width of the loop greater or less than its height? Instead of a smooth loop, do we have a "tail" constructed of two or three curves meeting to form sharp points (cusps)? Or do we have the entire letter formed by a continuous, unbroken curve without sharp changes of direction?

If a number of observers were asked to classify the letter *g* according to this scheme, I would not expect much variation in the results except in a few borderline cases. If one observer returned results widely different from the others, I would inquire into what he was doing wrong. You don't have to take my word for this. I ask you to examine the originals of these Letters in the British Library, going through them page by page in chronological order and deciding by direct observation whether there is evidence of:

(a) a *gradual* development of the KH style over a period of several years with the elimination of Blavatskian forms (Hodgson), or

(b) considerable variability of form in some of the characters in the first few Mahatma Letters received, a variability that was largely corrected in the course of the first fortnight without any obvious elimination of Blavatskian forms (Harrison).

Who is right, Hodgson or I?

*CRITIC*: Do I take the central issue of your study to be that you claim to demonstrate from an analysis of Madame Blavatsky's "ordinary" writing that she could not have been responsible for the KH Letters?

*VH*: No. The main issue is that the Hodgson Report is a BAD report that should never have been published, whoever its subject may have

64 / *H. P. Blavatsky and the SPR*

been. It is untrustworthy. If you ask, does it matter, after the passage of more than a century? I reply that it matters a great deal. The Hodgson Report is still accepted by many compilers of encyclopedias and dictionaries as the last word on Madame Blavatsky.

*CRITIC*: Since it is known that HPB wrote extensively in hands other than her own, your central claim is bound to collapse unless either (a) you can find specimens of the other writings and analyze them or (b) you can find reasons for denying that anybody, either as the result of practice or in trance (it doesn't matter which) can develop a style of writing so different from his normal writing that an expert (if I may use this term since you appear to be denying that there are any!) would fail to detect their common origin.

*VH*: I hold that as experts Hodgson, Netherclift, and Sims left a lot to be desired, and I have given my reasons for this opinion. There are good experts available, and you will find the names and addresses of some of them currently practicing in the UK Register of Expert Witnesses (JS Publications, Newmarket, Suffolk).

The only way we know that HPB wrote extensively in other hands is through the testimony of eyewitnesses whom Hodgson dismissed as credulous and unreliable. Chief of these is Olcott. If you accept Olcott's word, it is clear that HPB's writing in other styles was paranormal, not common fraud and imposture; and there was a case for HPB that was worth serious investigation.

Of course it is conceptually possible that HPB might have been able to perfect, by dint of much effort and practice, styles of writing and composition in which all evidence of her authorship was lost. I repeat that *there is no evidence of common origin* of the KH, M, and HPB scripts, and this means exactly what it says. Suspicions and remote, hypothetical, and unsubstantiated possibilities are not *evidence*. You cannot convict a person for forgery without hard evidence; and in English Law a person is presumed innocent until proved guilty. A "not proven" verdict is not allowed. Hodgson did claim abundant evidence of common origin of the HPB and KH scripts, and I still require to know what it is.

In all such problems which affect real life (and are not mere academic diversions) we have to distinguish between what is conceivably possible, however implausible and farfetched, and what is, in Eliza Doolittle's classic words, "not bloody likely."

Do, pray, remember that there are Letters which, as even Hodgson was forced to admit, HPB could not possibly have written, as she was too far away at the time and communications were bad. To circumvent this difficulty, HPB had (according to Hodgson) to train Damodar, and maybe others, to write with equal fluency in the KH style and to compose suitable letters for her while she was away. She had in addition to master the very different M writing and maintain the distinct differences in literary style between the KH and M Letters and her own. She would have to be able to compose original and consistent KH Letters of 16,000 words at a stretch without significant reversions to her normal style, in answer to specific questions on abstruse subjects.

And she did all this (according to Hodgson) in order to foment unrest against British rule in India.

Do you really believe this? I do not.

# Opinion

On the basis of the Hodgson Report itself and of the primary evidence available to me, I give it as my OPINION that:

1) The Hodgson Report is not a scientific study. It reads like part of a judicial inquiry recording only the address of the Counsel for the Prosecution. There is no address of a Counsel for the Defense, no cross-examination of the Prosecution's chief witnesses, no recall of Defense witnesses rejected by the Prosecution, and no Judge's summing up.

2) Richard Hodgson was either ignorant or contemptuous of the basic principles of English Justice. No court would accept his testimony.

3) In cases where it has been possible to check Hodgson's statements against the direct testimony of original documents, his statements are found to be either false or to have no significance in the context. This applies in particular to *Three Cardinal Statements* on which hangs his whole contention that Madame Blavatsky wrote the Mahatma Letters herself in a disguised hand in order to deceive.

4) Having read the Mahatma Letters in the holographs, I am left with the strong impression that the writers KH and M were real and distinct human beings. They had their fair share of prejudice and were influenced by the viewpoint of their time.

5) Who KH was I do not know, but I am of the opinion that all letters in the British Library initialed KH originated from him. The basic characteristics of his handwriting are present from first to last, but in the earliest letters in particular there are variations in and distortions of some of the characters. These variations do not bear the hallmark of the apprentice forger.

I am satisfied that the Mahatma Letters were not dictated to *chelas* who wrote them in their own handwriting. However, it is stated in the letters themselves that many of them were transmitted in KH's hand-

68 / H. P. Blavatsky and the SPR

writing by *chelas* using "precipitation" or what seems to be a human FAX process. If this suggestion is plausible, it could be that the *chelas* were having difficulty with the system at first, which had to be "debugged." Most of the "debugging" must have been done within a fortnight.

6) I draw attention to curious and unexplained features of the KH letters, namely the clear, regular striations of some of the writing apparently made with blue pencil (Fig. 11), the small amount of ink penetration even when thin "rice" paper was used, the unexplained features of the erasures seemingly made with ink eradicator yet without staining or roughening of the paper, the variability of some (but not all) of the characters and the (at times) grossly exaggerated t-bars. These features suggest that the documents preserved in the British Library may be *copies*, made by some unknown process, of originals which we do not possess.

7) It is almost certain that the incriminating Blavatsky-Coulomb letters have been lost or destroyed, but there is strong circumstantial evidence that these letters were forgeries made by Alexis and Emma Coulomb, who had strong motives and ample means for doing so.

8) I have found no evidence that the Mahatma Letters were written by Helena Blavatsky consciously and deliberately in a disguised form of her own handwriting developed over a period of several years, as claimed by Richard Hodgson. That is, I find no evidence of common origin between the KH, M, and HPB scripts. In any ordinary legal case I would regard them as different scripts and attribute them to different authors.

9) If any of the KH and M scripts came through the hand of Madame Blavatsky while she was in a state of trance, sleep, or other altered states of consciouness known to psychologists and psychiatrists, KH and M might be considered sub-personalities of Helena Blavatsky. To what extent the sub-personalities are independent is a matter for debate; but in no case would conscious fraud or imposture be involved. Nor does this supposition circumvent the difficulty that there are KH letters which even Hodgson had to admit Madame Blavatsky could not possibly have written as she was too far away at the time and communications were bad.

10) I am unable to express an opinion about the "phenomena" described in the first part of the Hodgson Report. All eyewitnesses and

*Opinion* / 69

items of firsthand evidence are gone, and I have no way of checking whether any of the reported "phenomena" were genuine; but having studied Hodgson's methods, I have come to distrust his account and explanation of the said "phenomena."

11) H. P. Blavatsky was known to be highly complex and hard to understand. There are still many unanswered questions concerning her life and work. However, I am of the opinion that in any future assessment of her, the "REPORT OF THE COMMITTEE APPOINTED TO INVESTIGATE PHENOMENA CONNECTED WITH THE THEOSOPHICAL SOCIETY," published in 1885 by the Society for Psychical Research, should be used with great caution, if not disregarded. It is badly flawed.

IN WITNESS WHEREOF I HAVE MADE MY AFFIDAVIT DATED THE 27th DAY OF FEBRUARY 1997, NOW LODGED WITH THE INTERNATIONAL HEADQUARTERS OF THE THEOSOPHICAL SOCIETY, PASADENA, CALIFORNIA, USA, A COPY OF WHICH HAS BEEN SENT TO THE SOCIETY FOR PSYCHICAL RESEARCH, LONDON, ENGLAND.

VERNON HARRISON

# AFFIDAVIT
(77% scale)

## AFFIDAVIT

**I, VERNON GEORGE WENTWORTH HARRISON**, of SOLE FARM HOUSE, 51 CHURCH ROAD, GREAT BOOKHAM, LEATHERHEAD, KT23 3PQ in the County of Surrey, England, Bachelor of Science, Doctor of Philosophy, Chartered Physicist and Chartered Engineer, Fellow of the Institute of Physics, Honorary Fellow and Past President of the Royal Photographic Society of Great Britain, Fellow of the Chartered Institution of Building Services Engineers, Fellow of the Royal Society of Arts and for the past twenty years professional examiner of questioned documents.

### MAKE OATH AND SAY

WHEREAS HELENA PETROVNA BLAVATSKY née HAHN (1831 - 1891) Founder of the Theosophical Society, was denounced in 1885 as 'one of the most accomplished, ingenious and interesting impostors in history' by THE REPORT OF THE COMMITTEE APPOINTED TO INVESTIGATE PHENOMENA CONNECTED WITH THE THEOSOPHICAL SOCIETY published by the Society for Psychical Research in its Proceedings, volume 3, pages 201 - 400 (1885), which report is commonly called and is hereinafter referred to as the Hodgson Report since the bulk of it was written by Richard Hodgson.

AND WHEREAS the said Hodgson Report has for more than a century been widely accepted by biographers and compilers of reference works as proof that the said Helena Petrovna Blavatsky knowingly engaged in fraudulent practices on an impressive scale.

AND WHEREAS there remains certain primary evidence relating to this case, that is to say The Mahatma Letters to A.P. Sinnett preserved in the British Library (Additional MSS 45284, 45285 & 45286), against which some of the statements made by Richard Hodgson in the Hodgson Report may be critically examined.

AND WHEREAS the said Mahatma Letters in the British Library comprise holograph letters from the following authors:
'KH' (one hundred and eight); 'M' (twenty six); Helena Blavatsky (nine); Subba Row (three, one with added comments by 'KH'); A.O. Hume (two); A.P.Sinnett (two); 'The Disinherited' (one); Stainton Moses (one); and Damodar (one).

I DECLARE THEREFORE that I have studied the Hodgson Report as a legal document and I have examined the said Mahatma Letters not only in the holographs preserved in the British Library but also in reproductions of the same prepared and supplied by the British Library in the form of a set of 1323 colour slides. I have examined microscopically each and every one of the 1323 slides found in a complete set, and wherever appropriate I have read the writing in a line-by-line scan at a magnification of x50 diameters.

I HAVE FOUND AND AFFIRM that:

(1)     The Hodgson Report is not a scientific study. It reads more like a portion of a judicial inquiry recording only the address of a Counsel for the Prosecution who has made up his mind in the early stages of the inquiry and thereafter is interested only in evidence, however dubious, that can be made to support his case. There is no address of a Counsel for the Defence, no cross-examination of the Prosecution's chief witnesses, no recall of Defence Witnesses rejected by the Prosecution and no Judge's summing up.

(2)     Richard Hodgson was either ignorant of or contemptuous of the basic principles of English justice. He quotes verbal and uncorroborated statements of unnamed witnesses. He cites documents that are neither reproduced in his report nor capable of identification. He advances conjecture as established fact. He importunes his handwriting experts until they give him the answers he wants. The possibility that someone other than Helena Blavatsky might have written the Mahatma Letters was never considered.

(3)     In cases where it has been possible to check Hodgson's statements against the direct testimony of original documents, his statements are found either to be false or to have no significance in the context. This applies in particular to Three Cardinal Statements on which hangs his whole contention that Helena Blavatsky wrote the Mahatma Letters herself in a disguised hand in order to deceive.

(4)     Having read the Mahatma Letters, I am left with the strong impression that the writers 'KH' and 'M' were real and distinct human beings, not demi-gods or 'shells'. They have their fair share of prejudice and are influenced by the viewpoint of their time.

(5)     I am of the opinion that all the letters initialled by 'KH' originated from him. The basic characteristics of his handwriting persist from first to last; but in the earliest letters in particular, there are variations in and distortions of some of the characters. These variations do not bear the hallmark of the apprentice forger. They seem to have been introduced by the method (unknown) of transmission of the Letters.

(6)     I draw attention to curious and unexplained features of the writing of the Mahatma Letters, that is to say: the regular, clear striations of some of the writing apparently written in blue pencil; the small amount of ink penetration even when thin 'rice' paper was used; the unexplained features of the erasures seemingly made with ink eradicator yet without staining or roughening of the paper; the variability of some (but not all) of the characters; and the (at times) grossly exaggerated t-bars. These features suggest that the documents preserved in the British Library may be copies, made by some unknown FAX process, of originals which we do not possess. Laboratory work on these scripts is desirable.

(7)    It is almost certain that the incriminating <u>Blavatsky-Coulomb Letters</u>, of which Hodgson makes much in his report, have been lost or destroyed. Few ever saw them. Helena Blavatsky was denied access to them. Hodgson gives no illustrations of them in his report. I have not been able to locate a reliable reproduction or even facsimile of any of them. There is strong circumstantial evidence that these letters (or at least the incriminating portions of them) were forgeries made by Alexis and Emma Coulomb who had both strong motives and ample means for doing so.

(8)    I have found no evidence that the Mahatma Letters preserved in the British Library were written by Helena Blavatsky consciously and deliberately in a disguised form of her own handwriting cultivated over a period of several years, as claimed by Richard Hodgson. That is to say, I find no evidence of common origin between the 'KH', 'M' and 'HPB' scripts. In any ordinary legal case I would regard them as different scripts and attribute them to three different persons.

(9)    If any of the 'KH' and 'M' scripts came through the hand of Helena Blavatsky while she was in a state of trance, sleep, multiple personality or other altered states of consciousness known to psychologists and psychiatrists, 'KH' and 'M' might be considered sub-personalities of Helena Blavatsky. To what extent the supposed sub-personalities are independent is a matter for debate; but in no case would conscious fraud or imposture be involved. Nor does this supposition circumvent the difficulty that there are 'KH' letters which even Richard Hodgson had to admit Helena Blavatsky could not possibly have written, as she was too far away at the time and communications were bad.

(10)    I am unable to express an opinion about the 'phenomena' described in the first part of the Hodgson report. All witnesses and items of first-hand evidence are gone and I have no way of checking whether any of the reported 'phenomena' were genuine; but, having studied Richard Hodgson's methods, I have come to distrust his account and explanation of the said 'phenomena'

Helena Petrovna Blavatsky's co-workers and acquaintances testify that she was of highly complex personality and hard to understand. There are still many unanswered questions concerning her life and work.

<u>BE IT KNOWN THEREFORE</u> that it is in my professional OPINION derived from a study of this case extending over a period of more than fifteen years, that future historians and biographers of the said Helena Petrova Blavatsky, the compilers of reference books, encyclopaedias and dictionaries, as well as the general public, should come to realise that THE REPORT OF THE COMMITTEE APPOINTED TO INVESTIGATE PHENOMENA CONNECTED WITH THE THEOSOPHICAL SOCIETY, published in 1885 by the Society for Psychical Research, should be read with great caution, if not disregarded. Far from being a model of impartial investigation so often claimed for it over more than a century, it is badly flawed and untrustworthy.

It is my intention to lodge this Affidavit for safe keeping with the International Headquarters of the Theosophical Society, Pasadena, California, USA and an attested copy with the Society for ~~Physical~~ Psychical Research, London , England.

| | |
|---|---|
| SWORN by the said VERNON | ) |
| GEORGE WENTWORTH HARRISON | )  *Vernon Harrison.* |
| at The Georgian House, | ) |
| Swan Mews, High Street, | ) |
| Leatherhead, Surrey, | ) |
| England this  27th  day | ) |
| of  February  1997 | ) |

Before me,

*JmH Graham*

J.M.H. GRAHAM

<u>A solicitor empowered to administer Oaths</u>

J.M.H. GRAHAM
SOLICITOR
THE GEORGIAN HOUSE
SWAN MEWS, HIGH STREET
LEATHERHEAD, SURREY

# About the Author

VERNON GEORGE WENTWORTH HARRISON was born in Sutton Coldfield, Warwickshire, England, in March 1912. His father was a schoolteacher specializing in French. Vernon was educated at Bishop Vesey's Grammar School, Sutton Coldfield, and at the University of Birmingham where he read physics, chemistry, and mathematics. After graduation he undertook three years of postgraduate study and research in the Department of Physics. In this study the use of photography and photomicrography as recording media played a prominent role.

After obtaining his Ph.D. he found employment as a research physicist in the Printing & Allied Trades Research Association (PATRA) with laboratories then located in London. His work at PATRA had hardly started when war broke out and he was put on to war work for the Ministry of Supply. PATRA lost all its records and scientific equipment in the last big fire raid on London, and it was not until 1947 that the staff was able to move into new laboratories at Leatherhead, about twenty miles south of London. Here he was able at last to start work on the optical properties of paper, color printing, and the quality of halftone reproduction. In 1957 he was appointed Director of Research of PATRA and was responsible for the administration of a staff which by then had grown to around 120.

In 1967 he moved to Thos. De La Rue & Co. in the capacity of Research Manager of their research center then located at Maidenhead. De La Rue prints banknotes (bills), postage stamps, stock certificates, passports, and other types of security documents; and an important part of the work of the research center was to study the methods of counterfeiters and forgers and to devise methods of improving the security of the Company's products.

This work aroused an interest in forged printed and written matter generally, so that on retirement in 1977 he was able to set up in private practice as an examiner of questioned documents. Being independent, he can work for either prosecution or defense. He is used to giving

78 / *About the Author*

evidence in Court and submitting to cross-examination. His work of recent years has covered a wide range of subjects from disputed Elizabethan documents to graffiti on walls, dubious wills, forged mortgage agreements and financial documents in profusion, anonymous and poison-pen letters, threatening notes, a spy case, examination of counterfeit currency and illicit printing plates, identification of banknote paper recovered from drains, and the evidential value of photographs. He considers this period to be the most interesting and, maybe, the most useful of his life.

He has had a lifelong interest in photography and from 1974 to 1976 he was President of the Royal Photographic Society of Great Britain. He has also had a lifelong interest in the music of Franz Liszt, and is the surviving co-founder and a past Chairman of the (English) Liszt Society.

The author describes himself as "reading the equations of Schrödinger and Dirac through the eyes of Francis Thompson."